Insulin Resistance

How to Prevent and Reverse Insulin Resistance and improve your health.

Easy recipes to control diabetes and combat kidney disease.

Mary K. Morgan

Table of Contents

Introduction _____1

Chapter 1: Insulin Resistance _____3

Chapter 2: Natural Ways to Improve Your Insulin
Sensitivity_____15

Chapter 3: Lifestyle Changes to Reduce Insulin
Resistance _____20

Chapter 4: The Insulin Resistance Diet _____24

Chapter 5: Breakfast Recipes _____38

Chapter 6: Lunch Recipes _____69

Chapter 7: Side Dish Recipes _____101

Chapter 8: Snack and Appetizer Recipes _____131

Chapter 9: Fish and Seafood Recipes _____163

Chapter 10: Poultry Recipes _____195

Chapter 11: Meat Recipes_____228

Chapter 12: Vegetable Recipes _____263

Chapter 13: Dessert Recipes_____286

Chapter 14: Condiments, Sauces, Dressings _____316

Conclusion _____350

Recipes Index _____351

Introduction

Scientific studies show that Americans are slowly becoming ill from an impaired glucose metabolism, that manifests itself as a chronic condition known as insulin resistance. Being diagnosed with insulin resistance can be scary. However, it is also an opportunity to improve your health and get yourself in better shape than ever. Recent data shows that around 70 to 80 million Americans have insulin resistance, with tens of millions more estimated to have prediabetes and not know it.

These are alarming numbers and you might be scared and confused. However, there is a flipside; it also means that you have caught insulin resistance before it is too late and you develop diabetes. There are steps you can take to improve your health and reverse insulin resistance. This comprehensive insulin resistance guide will reveal what steps to take and empower you to find the healthy eating and lifestyle changes that work best for you to reverse insulin resistance. It's time to feel better and get healthy by following a simple step-by-step plan for a healthy lifestyle.

Whether you have been diagnosed with insulin resistance, prediabetes, diabetes, or obesity, and want to lose weight and become insulin sensitive again, this book is for you. Written by a nutritionist, this book walks you through practical ways to cook and eat for insulin resistance with delicious recipes. In this book, you will learn about everything you need to become more insulin sensitive. Learn to live a healthy, energetic lifestyle even if you are diagnosed with insulin resistance.

Chapter 1: Insulin Resistance

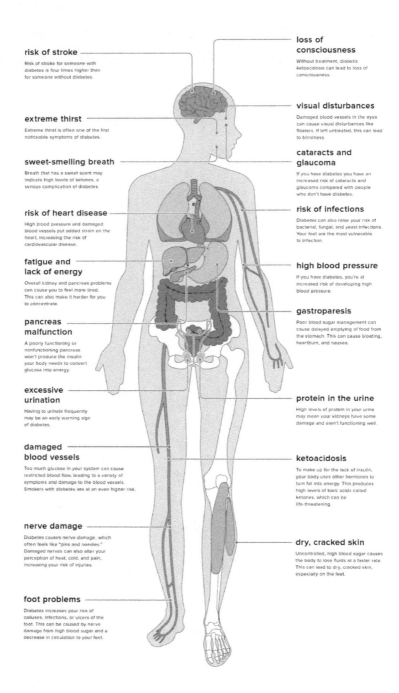

risk of stroke

Risk of stroke for someone with diabetes is four times higher than for someone without diabetes.

extreme thirst

Extreme thirst is often one of the first noticeable symptoms of diabetes.

sweet-smelling breath

Breath that has a sweet scent may indicate high levels of ketones, a serious complication of diabetes.

risk of heart disease

High blood pressure and damaged blood vessels put added strain on the heart, increasing the risk of cardiovascular disease.

fatigue and lack of energy

Overall kidney and pancreas problems can cause you to feel more tired. This can also make it harder for you to concentrate.

pancreas malfunction

A poorly functioning or nonfunctioning pancreas won't produce the insulin your body needs to convert glucose into energy.

excessive urination

Having to urinate frequently may be an early warning sign of diabetes.

damaged blood vessels

Too much glucose in your system can cause restricted blood flow, leading to a variety of symptoms and damage to the blood vessels. Smokers with diabetes are at an even higher risk.

nerve damage

Diabetes causes nerve damage, which often feels like "pins and needles." Damaged nerves can also alter your perception of heat, cold, and pain, increasing your risk of injuries.

foot problems

Diabetes increases your risk of calluses, infections, or ulcers of the foot. This can be caused by nerve damage from high blood sugar and a decrease in circulation to your feet.

loss of consciousness

Without treatment, diabetic ketoacidosis can lead to loss of consciousness.

visual disturbances

Damaged blood vessels in the eyes can cause visual disturbances like floaters. If left untreated, this can lead to blindness.

cataracts and glaucoma

If you have diabetes you have an increased risk of cataracts and glaucoma compared with people who don't have diabetes.

risk of infections

Diabetes can also raise your risk of bacterial, fungal, and yeast infections. Your feet are the most vulnerable to infection.

high blood pressure

If you have diabetes, you're at increased risk of developing high blood pressure.

gastroparesis

Poor blood sugar management can cause delayed emptying of food from the stomach. This can cause bloating, heartburn, and nausea.

protein in the urine

High levels of protein in your urine may mean your kidneys have some damage and aren't functioning well.

ketoacidosis

To make up for the lack of insulin, your body uses other hormones to turn fat into energy. This produces high levels of toxic acids called ketones, which can be life-threatening.

dry, cracked skin

Uncontrolled, high blood sugar causes the body to lose fluids at a faster rate. This can lead to dry, cracked skin, especially on the feet.

Type 2 diabetes is a chronic condition that affects the way your body metabolizes blood sugar/glucose.

Symptoms

Here are the signs and symptoms of insulin resistance and type 2 diabetes:

- Areas of darkened skin, usually in the neck and armpits

- Frequent infections

- Slow-healing sores

- Blurred vision

- Fatigue

- Unintended weight loss

- Increased hunger

- Frequent urination

- Increased thirst

Causes

A person develops insulin resistance and type 2 diabetes when their body is unable to produce enough insulin or becomes resistant to insulin.

Risk factors of insulin resistance and type 2 diabetes include:

- Being obese or overweight

- High blood pressure

- Low levels of good cholesterol and elevated levels of bad cholesterol

- Sedentary lifestyle

- Family history

- Increasing age

- Impaired glucose tolerance

- Polycystic ovary syndrome

- Gestational diabetes during pregnancy

- Ethnic background: Asian-Americans, Native Americans, African-Americans, Hispanic/Latino Americans, Pacific Islanders, and Alaskan natives are at greater risk.

Many factors contribute to insulin resistance, but one factor that is believed to heighten the risk is the increased fat levels in the blood. Various studies show that high fatty acids in the blood cause insulin resistance.

- https://www.ncbi.nlm.nih.gov/pubmed/15919784

- https://onlinelibrary.wiley.com/doi/full/10.1046/j.1365-2362.32.s3.3.x

- https://www.ncbi.nlm.nih.gov/pubmed/11347757

Eating too much and carrying excess body fat is the main reasons for excess fatty acids in the blood. Studies show that weight gain and obesity are all linked to insulin resistance.

- https://www.ncbi.nlm.nih.gov/pubmed/20547978

- https://www.ncbi.nlm.nih.gov/pubmed/18171910

Other causes of insulin resistance include

1. Consuming fructose. Eating food items with added sugar is linked to insulin resistance.

2. Inflammation. Inflammation in your body can lead to insulin resistance.

3. Inactivity. Studies show living a sedentary lifestyle causes insulin resistance and physical activity increases insulin sensitivity.

4. Gut microbiota. The absence of healthy gut bacteria can cause insulin resistance.

Common differences between type 1 and type 2 diabetes

Type 1 Diabetes	Type 2 Diabetes
Usually diagnosed in childhood	Generally diagnosed after the age of 30
No link with excess body weight	Usually associated with extra body weight
Higher levels of ketones at diagnosis	Usually associated with high cholesterol and/or high blood pressure at diagnosis
Treated with an insulin pump or insulin injections	Initially treated without medication
Cannot be controlled without taking insulin	Occasionally, patients can avoid taking medication and live healthily

Insulin

Many people don't have a clear idea about insulin. Insulin is a hormone that is vital to our health. However, in the wrong amounts it can be deadly. It is life-saving for those with type 1 diabetes but can speed up the progress to type 2 diabetes and obesity for those with poor diets.

Insulin is the body's way to regulate glucose in the bloodstream, which when it has an excess in toxic amounts, sends it to the only two other places in the body where it can be stored - the muscles or the liver. Glucose is one of the main sources of energy for the human body, but the human body can only store a finite amount of glucose.

The pancreas of the human body produces insulin in response to ingested sugar; even some sugar substitutes can activate a small insulin response. The insulin mixes in the bloodstream and links with cells and unlocks them, allowing those cells to absorb glucose for immediate use or to make their own stores of longer-lasting glycogen. It also allows cells to better absorb amino acids.

Insulin prompts the liver to store glycogen and if there is any extra, it gets converted into body fat. Absence of insulin has the opposite effect. The liver breaks down glycogen into glucose and excretes it for the body to use.

Insulin resistance

For the human body, glucose is the preferred choice of energy. When we eat carbohydrate, it is broken down to create glucose. The additional glucose gets stored as glycogen in the body. Our muscles will use any readily available glucose first and then use it stores of glycogen. When insulin comes around to distribute glucose our cells use that energy, but also take enough glucose to replenish their stores of glycogen.

Insulin's rather elegant system for storing toxic glucose in the muscle and liver doesn't function so well when the body is frequently exposed to high levels of blood glucose. Frequent or prolonged spikes in blood glucose can cause the body's cells to become resistant to insulin. When our glycogen stores are mostly full and a cell's energy requirement is low, then the cell will not be receptive to any insulin because it doesn't need glucose.

This leads to a resistance to insulin as the connections normally used to accept it begin changing and it becomes difficult for cells to accept insulin, even if they really need glucose. Repeated levels of high insulin secretion were not normal for our prehistoric ancestors.

The intended role of insulin in the body was to signal to the muscles and other cells to fill up their depleted stores of glycogen and use the glucose available. When insulin was released, the cells usually needed that glucose and gladly opened up to receive the glucose. If we fill those stores and don't use them, then when insulin comes to deliver some glucose those cells can't take in any more glucose and become resistant to insulin.

Too much insulin can cause problems, especially when cells become resistant. Insulin will convert glucose to visceral fat as a last option. This fat surrounds the internal organs at first and then grows around the abdomen. As fat grows by adipose cells accepting and converting glucose into fat, they can also reach a point where they have a difficult time accepting any more and become insulin themselves. With nowhere to go, the glucose usually ends up being converted to LDL cholesterol and wanders in the blood, clogging arteries.

How insulin resistance makes us fat

The hormone insulin is the important regulator of your blood glucose levels. Insulin is a hormone just like thyroid, estrogen, testosterone, or cortisone, and is secreted into your bloodstream by the pancreas gland. After you eat, digest, and absorb carbohydrate-rich foods, your blood glucose levels rise. So your body releases insulin. The insulin then transports glucose into your body cells to use as energy. If you have more glucose in your body than your cells need, insulin takes the extra blood glucose and transports it into fat storage. Blood sugar then returns to normal. This step is important because high levels of blood glucose are toxic to the body.

Insulin's main job is to regulate blood glucose, and insulin also signals fat storage. When insulin rises and spikes to regulate high blood sugar levels, more fat is also being stored. High insulin levels on a frequent basis will make you fat. You don't know this but the human body makes fat quickly - two to three hours after eating carb-rich food. So you may be thinking if insulin levels make you fat, then lower insulin levels make you thin. The answer is yes, low insulin levels will make you thin.

Diabetes

Insulin resistance can lead to diabetes later in life. The type of diabetes caused by insulin resistance is called type 2 diabetes. One of the popular theories about how insulin resistance can lead to diabetes is that the insulin supply from the pancreas eventually wears out from all of the challenging years of compensating for high-carb foods. Without insulin from the pancreas to control it, blood sugar levels rise. Uncontrolled high blood sugar levels (diabetes) cause significant damage to all body's organs but especially the kidneys, eyes, liver, blood vessels, and heart. Heart disease and blood vessel damage caused by diabetes are the most common killers of Americans today.

Diagnosing insulin resistance

There is not a single test existing that you can do to diagnose insulin resistance. There are a group of tests suggested including waist circumference measurements, fasting glucose levels, fasting insulin levels, glucose tolerance tests, and glucose-insulin tolerance tests.

Waist circumference

This is easy to do. For men, a waist measurement of more than forty inches strongly indicates insulin resistance. For women, a waist measurement of more than thirty-five inches is an indicator.

Fasting glucose levels

This is a very common simple blood test that is often done to test insulin resistance. It measures glucose levels after you have fasted for several hours. If this blood sugar level is slightly higher than normal, (normal glucose is 80 to 100 mg/dl) but not in the diabetic range, you are said to have impaired glucose tolerance. This strongly suggests insulin resistance.

Fasting insulin levels

Like fasting glucose, levels of insulin are measured in the blood after fasting. If levels are elevated, insulin resistance is likely to be a problem. A fasting insulin level higher than 10 uIU/ml is a flag for insulin resistance.

Glucose tolerance tests and glucose-insulin tolerance tests

These tests are more complicated and more costly than fasting tests because they require patients to take repeated blood tests over several hours. This combined glucose-insulin tolerance test is the best indicator of insulin resistance.

American Association of Clinical Endocrinologists Clinical Criteria for Diagnosis of Insulin-Resistance Syndrome

1. BMI greater than 25

2. Triglycerides greater than 150 mg/dl

3. HDL cholesterol levels

- less than 40 mg/dl for men

- less than 50 mg/dl for women

4. Blood pressure greater than 130/85 mm Hg

5. Two-hour glucose challenge higher than 140 mg/dl

6. Fasting glucose between 110 and 126 mg/dl

Chapter 2: Natural Ways to Improve Your Insulin Sensitivity

Here are a few natural, science-backed ways to boost your insulin sensitivity.

1. Get more sleep: Studies show that a brief amount of sleep or an irregular sleep pattern can increase your risk of heart disease and diabetes. Various studies have also associated poor sleep with reduced insulin sensitivity.

- https://www.ncbi.nlm.nih.gov/pubmed/10898125

- https://www.ncbi.nlm.nih.gov/pubmed/20371664

2. Exercise more: Regular exercise can help you increase insulin sensitivity. Many studies show the benefits of exercise among men and women with or without diabetes. Exercises that burn more calories such as resistance training and high intensity interval training (HIIT) are recommended by doctors.

- https://www.ncbi.nlm.nih.gov/pubmed/10683091

- https://www.ncbi.nlm.nih.gov/pubmed/15628572

- https://www.ncbi.nlm.nih.gov/pubmed/26486356

3. Reduce Stress: Living a stressful life affects your body's

ability to regulate blood sugar. Activities like sleep, exercise, and meditation are great ways to reduce stress and increase insulin sensitivity.

• https://www.ncbi.nlm.nih.gov/pmc/articles/ PMC3050109/

• https://www.ncbi.nlm.nih.gov/pubmed/1605044

4. Lose weight: Losing belly fat will help you increase insulin sensitivity. Many studies show a link between lower insulin sensitivity and higher amounts of belly fat.

• https://www.ncbi.nlm.nih.gov/pmc/articles/ PMC4038351/

• https://physoc.onlinelibrary.wiley.com/doi/full/ 10.1113/jphysiol.2009.175489

5. Eat more soluble fiber: Soluble fiber offers many benefits, including reducing appetite and lowering cholesterol. Many studies also show a link between increased insulin sensitivity and high soluble fiber intake. Also, soluble fiber can boost the production of gut-friendly bacteria in your gut. Studies show gut-friendly bacteria increase insulin sensitivity. Foods such as flaxseeds, oatmeal, legumes, Brussels sprouts, and oranges are rich with soluble fiber.

- https://www.ncbi.nlm.nih.gov/pubmed/23218116

- https://www.nature.com/articles/nature18646

6. Add more colorful fruit and vegetables to your diet: Many studies show that a diet rich in plant compounds is linked to higher insulin sensitivity.

- https://www.ncbi.nlm.nih.gov/pmc/articles/PMC4073986/

- https://www.ncbi.nlm.nih.gov/pmc/articles/PMC4852413/

7. Use more herbs and spices: Herbs and spices such as garlic, ginger, turmeric, and fenugreek can increase insulin sensitivity. Fenugreek seeds are rich with soluble fiber, turmeric contains curcumin, and various studies show that adding ginger and garlic in dishes increases insulin sensitivity.

- https://www.ncbi.nlm.nih.gov/pubmed/19665995

- https://www.ncbi.nlm.nih.gov/pmc/articles/PMC2243241/

- https://www.ncbi.nlm.nih.gov/pubmed/22828920

8. Use cinnamon: Studies show that cinnamon can increase insulin sensitivity. Some studies even show that

compounds present in cinnamon can mimic insulin.

- https://www.ncbi.nlm.nih.gov/pmc/articles/PMC2901047/

- https://www.ncbi.nlm.nih.gov/pubmed/9762007

9. Green tea: Studies show that drinking green tea can reduce blood sugar and increase insulin sensitivity.

- https://www.ncbi.nlm.nih.gov/pmc/articles/PMC3948786/

- https://www.ncbi.nlm.nih.gov/pubmed/23803878

- https://www.ncbi.nlm.nih.gov/pubmed/18496818

10. Apple cider vinegar: Studies show that vinegar can help increase insulin sensitivity.

- https://care.diabetesjournals.org/content/27/1/281

- https://www.ncbi.nlm.nih.gov/pubmed/27213723

11. Cut down on carbs: It is carbs that trigger blood glucose release and cause insulin levels to rise. Lowering your carb intake could help increase insulin sensitivity.

- https://www.ncbi.nlm.nih.gov/pmc/articles/PMC3608918/

- https://www.sciencedirect.com/science/article/pii/

S13190016415000766

12.Avoid trans-fats: Completely avoid artificial trans-fats. Animal studies show that there is a link between high trans-fat consumption and poor insulin resistance.

- https://www.ncbi.nlm.nih.gov/pubmed/17636085

- https://www.ncbi.nlm.nih.gov/pubmed/15789505

13.Lower your added sugar consumption: Added sugars are loaded with fructose and can lower insulin sensitivity. Avoid foods like pastries, cookies, cakes, candy, sugar-sweetened beverages, and highly processed foods.

- https://www.ncbi.nlm.nih.gov/pubmed/17921363

- https://nutritionandmetabolism.biomedcentral.com/articles/10.1186/1743-7075-2-5

14.Add a supplement: Evidence suggest that resveratrol, magnesium, bebeerine, and chromium can increase insulin sensitivity.

- https://www.ncbi.nlm.nih.gov/pubmed/15208835

- https://www.ncbi.nlm.nih.gov/pubmed/12663588

- https://www.ncbi.nlm.nih.gov/pmc/articles/PMC3722087/

- https://www.ncbi.nlm.nih.gov/pubmed/25445538

Chapter 3: Lifestyle Changes to Reduce Insulin Resistance

Here are ways you can reduce insulin resistance:

1. Exercise: Daily physical activity is the easiest way to improve insulin sensitivity. Exercise will give you an immediate benefit.

2. Lose belly fat: Losing belly fat that surrounds your main organs is another effective way to reduce insulin resistance.

3. Quit smoking: Data shows that smoking can cause insulin resistance. Quit smoking.

4. Reduce sugar intake: Avoid added sugar-rich beverages.

5. Omega-3 fatty acids: Omega-3 fatty acids lower insulin resistance. Best sources of omega-3 fatty acids include flaxseeds, chia seeds, walnuts, soybeans, salmon, mackerel, sardines, anchovies, caviar, herring, oysters, and cod liver oil.

6. Supplements: Supplements such as Bebeerine (https://www.amazon.com/s?k=berberine&ref=nb_sb_noss) can boost insulin sensitivity and reduce blood sugar. Magnesium supplements can also help.

7. Sleep: Studies show that poor sleep habits can cause insulin resistance. Improving sleep quality can help you improve insulin resistance. Tips on better sleep:

• Maintain a fixed bedtime: Fix a bedtime and maintain it regularly even on weekends. Go to bed when you normally feel tired and sleepy, and go to bed at exactly the same time daily. If you have to adjust your bedtime, make small changes like going to bed 10 or 20 minutes early or late.

• Turn off your computer and TV before bed: Don't play stimulating games or watch violent TV shows before bedtime. These stimulating activities delay the sleeping process. Listen to soft music or read a book instead.

• Use an e-reader and don't use backlit devices such as iPads for reading.

• Keep your bedroom dark and cool, ideally around 18 C.

• Use a comfortable bed or bed mattress

• Use your bed only for sleep and sex

Things you should avoid before sleep

• Don't eat a heavy dinner just before bedtime. This will inhibit digestion and make you feel sick afterward.

• Avoid drinking alcohol before sleep. Alcohol before

bedtime leads to shallow sleep.

• Avoid caffeine and smoking before bedtime, and don't take sleeping pills.

• Reduce stress: Data shows that reducing stress can help you improve insulin resistance. Here are ways to reduce stress:

Talk with a friend	Spend time in nature or walk in the park
Do some exercise	Read a good book
Look at memory or storyboards	Watch a favorite film
Take some photos or paint	Daydream for 10 minutes
Listen to a radio program and keep your eyes closed	Listen to your favorite music
Listen to some soothing sound, like rainfall	Play a relaxation CD
Do some baking	Burn some aromatic oil
Light a scented candle	Drink a cup of tea
Sing a song	Laugh
Read affirmations loudly	Chew sugarless gum
Eat a piece of dark chocolate	Use deep breathing exercises
Squeeze a stress ball	Do some yoga
Have a massage	Stroke a pet
Wear soft, warm clothing	

9. Donate blood: Studies show that donating blood can improve insulin sensitivity. The reason is high levels of iron in the blood are linked with insulin resistance.

10.Intermittent fasting: Following this eating plan is very effective in improving insulin sensitivity.

Low-carb diets

Low-carb diets fight metabolic syndrome and insulin resistance and type 2 diabetes. Studies show that following a low carb diet instead of a regular diet is beneficial for insulin resistance.

- https://www.ncbi.nlm.nih.gov/pmc/articles/PMC2633336/

- https://www.ncbi.nlm.nih.gov/pmc/articles/PMC1325029/

- https://www.ncbi.nlm.nih.gov/pubmed/15616799

- https://www.ncbi.nlm.nih.gov/pubmed/15047685

- https://www.ncbi.nlm.nih.gov/pubmed/24015695

Chapter 4: The Insulin Resistance Diet

Energy from Glucose (Carbohydrates)

Diets rich in carbohydrates cause your body to rely on glucose as the primary source of energy. What isn't used right away is stored in adipose (fat) tissue, causing fluctuations in energy levels and weight gain.

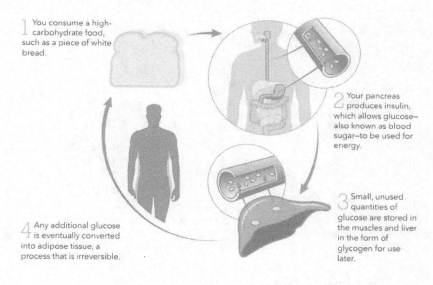

1 You consume a high-carbohydrate food, such as a piece of white bread.

2 Your pancreas produces insulin, which allows glucose—also known as blood sugar—to be used for energy.

3 Small, unused quantities of glucose are stored in the muscles and liver in the form of glycogen for use later.

4 Any additional glucose is eventually converted into adipose tissue, a process that is irreversible.

Carb-rich diet

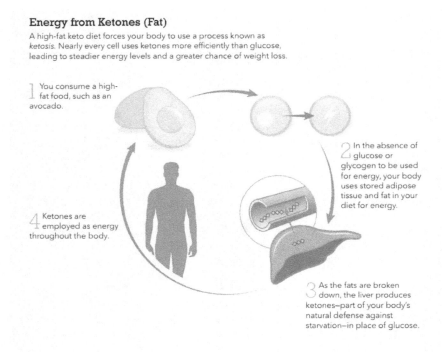

Energy from Ketones (Fat)

A high-fat keto diet forces your body to use a process known as *ketosis*. Nearly every cell uses ketones more efficiently than glucose, leading to steadier energy levels and a greater chance of weight loss.

1 You consume a high-fat food, such as an avocado.

2 In the absence of glucose or glycogen to be used for energy, your body uses stored adipose tissue and fat in your diet for energy.

4 Ketones are employed as energy throughout the body.

3 As the fats are broken down, the liver produces ketones—part of your body's natural defense against starvation—in place of glucose.

Ketogenic diet

Eating excessive carb-rich foods flood your bloodstream with glucose. Habitual eating of carb-rich foods gradually makes your body insulin resistant. So you need to follow a low-carb diet such as a Ketogenic diet. If you eat a low-carb, Ketogenic diet, you will eat fewer carbs and your blood will have less blood glucose. So your body doesn't have to produce a huge amount of insulin to remove glucose from the blood. Low insulin production will make your body sensitive to insulin again.

Now we are going to discuss what you can eat and have to avoid on the Ketogenic diet. You can eat from the following food groups:

• Fats and Oils: Get your fats from meat and nuts. Supplement with monounsaturated and saturated fats like olive oil, butter, and coconut oil.

• Protein: Whenever possible, eat grass-fed, pasture-raised, organic meat. Eat meat in moderation.

• Vegetables: Focus on eating vegetables that grow above the ground, mainly leafy green vegetables.

• Dairy: Focus on buying full-fat dairy products.

• Nuts and seeds: Eat fat-rich nuts such as almond and macadamia.

• Beverages: Stick to drinking mostly water. You can flavor it with lemon/ lime juice and stevia-based flavorings.

Let's discuss in detail:

Fats and Oils

• Saturated fats: Consume lard, coconut oil, ghee, and butter.

• Monounsaturated fats: avocado, olive, and macadamia nut oils.

• Polyunsaturated fats: Eat naturally occurring polyunsaturated fats such as fatty fish and fat from animal protein. Avoid processed polyunsaturated fat such as margarine spreads.

• Trans-fats: Completely avoid.

Protein

Here are the best proteins for you:

• Fish: Eat wild-caught fish like trout, snapper, salmon, mackerel, halibut, cod, tuna, and catfish. Fattier fish is better.

• Shellfish: Mussels, squid, scallops, crab, lobster, oysters, clams

• Whole eggs: Free-range from the local market

• Beef: Fatty cuts of steak, stew meat, roasts, ground beef

• Pork: Ham, tenderloin, pork chops, pork loin, ground beef

• Poultry: Wild game, chicken, quail, pheasant, duck

• Offal/Organ: Tongue, kidney, liver, heart

• Other meat: Wild game, turkey, veal, lamb, goat

• Bacon and Sausage: Avoid sugar or extra filler added items

• Nut Butter: Buy natural, unsweetened nuts and choose fattier versions like macadamia or almond nut butter

Vegetables and Fruit

Mostly eat vegetables that are low in carbs and high in nutrients. Focus on cruciferous vegetables that are leafy, green and grown above ground.

Limit the listed vegetables and fruits:

• Nightshades: peppers, eggplant, and tomato

• Root vegetables: Squash, mushrooms, garlic, parsnip, and onion

• Berries: Blueberries, blackberries, and raspberries

- Citrus: Orange, lemon, and lime

- Try to avoid starchy vegetables, bananas, and potatoes

Dairy Products

Here are some examples of dairy you can eat on the keto diet:

- Hard cheese, including Swiss, Parmesan, feta, aged cheddar, etc.

- Soft cheese, including Monterey Jack, Colby, blue, brie, mozzarella, etc.

- Spreadable cheese, including Crème Fraiche, mascarpone, sour cream, cream cheese, cottage cheese, etc.

- Homemade mayonnaise

- Heavy whipping cream

- Greek yogurt

Nuts and Seeds

- Low carb, fat-rich nuts: Pecans, Brazil nuts, macadamia nuts

• Moderate carb, fat-rich nuts: Peanuts, hazelnuts, almonds, walnuts, pine nuts

• High carb nuts: Avoid cashews and pistachios because they are high in carb.

Water and Beverages

Here is a list of beverages that Keto allows:

• Water: Drink more than 8 glasses of water daily

• Broth: Broth is important for Keto dieters. These are loaded with vitamins; nutrition and help replace electrolytes.

• You can drink tea and coffee.

• Choose unsweetened variations of almond and coconut milk.

• Avoid or severely reduce diet soda.

• Flavorings such as stevia and sucralose are fine.

• Choose hard liquor and avoid beer and wine because of high carb content.

Spices

Cayenne Pepper	Chili Powder
Cinnamon	Cumin
Oregano	Basil
Cilantro	Parsley
Rosemary	Thyme

Condiments and Sauces

Keto-friendly condiments include

- Syrups flavored with acceptable sweeteners

- Unsweetened, fatty salad dressing

- Worcestershire sauce

- Horseradish

- Low or no sugar added relish

- Low or no sugar added sauerkraut

- Cage-free mayonnaise

- Hot sauce

- Mustard

• Low or no sugar added ketchup

Try to avoid pre-made condiments

Sweeteners

Keto recommended sweeteners

• Stevia.

• Sucralose.

• Erythritol.

• Monk fruit

• Xylitol in moderation

Foods to avoid

• Sugar: Typically found in ice cream, chocolate, candy, sports drinks, juice, and soda. Avoid sugar completely.

• Grains: Avoid bread, buns, rice, corn, pastries, cakes, cereal, pasta, and beer. Avoid whole grains, including quinoa, buckwheat, barley, rye, and wheat.

• Starch: Avoid vegetables like yams and potatoes and other things like muesli and oats.

- Trans-Fats: Avoid them completely.

- Fruit: Avoid large fruits that are high in sugar (bananas, oranges, apples)

- Low-fat foods: Low-fat foods are high in carb and sugar. Avoid them.

Some health situations can make it difficult for you to follow the diet, including:

- People who are naturally very thin

- People who are prone to kidney stones

- People who have developed a pancreatic problem

- People with anorexia

- Women who are pregnant or breastfeeding

- People with rare metabolic disorders

- People with gallbladder disease

Keto Side effects and solutions

The common Keto side effects and the solutions:

1. Frequent Urination: This is nothing serious and goes

away on its own after a few days.

2. Dizziness and drowsiness: Potassium deficiency causes this problem. You can deal with these symptoms if you are prepared. Eat foods rich in potassium, such as:

• Avocados

• Meat, poultry, and fish

• Dairy

• Broccoli

• 2 cups of leafy greens daily

• Add salt to your meals and drink bone broth

• If necessary, you can take a 400mg magnesium supplement before bed.

3. Low Blood Sugar: Low blood sugar is another common Keto side effect. The symptoms go away on their own after a few days. To solve it:

• Eat every 3 to 4 hours. This will keep your blood sugar balanced.

• Drink organic broths or a high-quality electrolyte drink.

• Mineral-rich foods and foods that keep you hydrated. Eat cucumbers, celery, and Sea Snax.

• Take magnesium supplements. Take L-threonate in the 1-gram dose three times daily between meals.

4. Constipation: Eat more fiber-rich foods (non-starchy vegetables), drink lots of water and get enough salt. Also, you can take 400mg of magnesium supplement.

5. Diarrhea: Some people may experience diarrhea. To prevent it, don't skip on your fats. Before eating a meal, take a tsp. of sugar-free Metamucil or psyllium husk powder.

• Flu-Like Symptoms: Keto flu should go away on its own within a few days. Eating enough fat, staying hydrated and increasing salt intake can help prevent Keto flu. Drink broth daily.

• Bad Breath: Bad breath is the sign that your body is in Ketosis. You can increase water intake, slightly increase carbs or use a breath fresher to prevent bad breath.

• Muscle cramps: Taking a magnesium supplement to fix the issue.

• Heart Palpitations: You may notice a slight increase in heart rate in the first weeks of eating a low-carb diet. Drink more water and add salt to your foods. You can take a high-quality magnesium supplement and a multivitamin containing selenium and zinc to replace any nutrients lost during adaptation.

Some more tips

1. Try intermittent fasting. Practice intermittent fasting while you follow this diet plan. It will help you lose weight.

2. Lower stress: Living a stressful life can prevent your weight loss efforts. So lower stress.

3. Sleep well. Poor sleep can trigger stress, which will slow down fat burning.

4. Add more salt to your diet: You need to consume more salt when you follow a healthy low carb diet plan.

5. Exercise daily: Daily exercise will help you lose more weight.

6. Avoid sugar substitutes: Sugar substitutes can increase your sugar cravings.

7. Drink water: Your body needs more water with a low carb diet plan. Drink 8 to 10 big glasses of water daily.

8. Get your carbs from vegetables. Vegetables provide you with nutrients, fibers, and improve your gut health.

9. Use MCT oil: Using MCT oil can help you enter ketosis

sooner and stay in ketosis.

10.Avoid constipation: Constipation is a problem for beginners. Eat more fiber-rich foods and drink more water to avoid constipation.

11.Don't eat too much protein: Eating too much protein can stop your weight loss efforts.

12.Cook in batches: Cooking can be difficult for beginners. So cook in batches and freeze meals.

Chapter 5: Breakfast Recipes

Breakfast Muffins

Prep Time: 10 minutes

Cook Time: 30 minutes

Serving: 4

Ingredients

- Almond milk – ½ cup

- Eggs – 6

- Coconut oil - 1 tbsp.

- Salt and ground pepper to taste

- Kale – ¼ cup, chopped

- Prosciutto slices – 8

- Fresh chives – ¼ cup, chopped

Method

1. In a bowl, mix eggs with salt, pepper, milk, chives, and kale.

2. Grease a muffin tray with coconut oil, line with prosciutto slices, and pour in the egg mixture.

3. Place in the oven and bake at 350F for 30 minutes.

4. Cool and serve.

Nutritional Facts Per Serving

- Calories: 257

- Fat: 19.5g

- Carb: 3.4g

- Protein: 18.1g

Vegetable Breakfast Bread

Prep Time: 10 minutes

Cook Time: 25 minutes

Serving: 7

Ingredients

- Cauliflower head – 1, separated into florets

- Fresh parsley – ½ cup, chopped

- Spinach – 1 cup, torn

- Onion – 1, peeled and chopped

- Coconut oil – 1 tbsp.

- Pecans – ½ cup, ground

- Eggs – 3

- Garlic – 2 cloves and minced

- Salt and ground black pepper to taste

Method

1. In a food processor, mix cauliflower florets with salt, pepper, and pulse well.

2. Heat a pan with oil over medium heat.

3. Add cauliflower, onion, garlic, salt, and pepper. Stir-fry for 10 minutes.

4. In a bowl, mix eggs with salt, pepper, parsley, spinach, nuts, and stir well.

5. Add cauliflower mixture and stir well.

6. Spread mixture into forms placed on a baking sheet.

7. Heat oven to 350F and bake for 15 minutes.

8. Serve.

Nutritional Facts Per Serving

- Calories: 105

- Fat: 8.2g

- Carb: 5.2g

- Protein: 4.2g

Avocado Muffins

Prep Time: 10 minutes

Cook Time: 20 minutes

Serving: 12

Ingredients

- Eggs – 4

- Bacon slices – 6, chopped

- Onion – 1, peeled and chopped

- Coconut milk – 1 cup

- Avocado – 2 cups, pitted, peeled and chopped

- Salt and ground pepper to taste

- Baking soda – ½ tsp.

- Coconut flour – ½ cup

Method

1. Heat a pan over medium heat.

2. Add onion, bacon, and stir-fry for few minutes.

3. Mash the avocado in a bowl and whisk in eggs.

4. Add salt, milk, pepper, baking soda, coconut flour, and stir.

5. Add bacon mixture and stir again.

6. Grease a muffin tray with coconut oil.

7. Divide the eggs and avocado mixture into the tray.

8. Place in an oven at 350F, and bake for 20 minutes.

9. Serve.

Nutritional Facts Per Serving

- Calories: 175

- Fat: 15.1g

- Carb: 4.8g

- Protein: 6.5g

Cheese and Oregano Muffins

Prep Time: 10 minutes

Cook Time: 25 minutes

Serving: 6

Ingredients

- Olive oil - 2 tbsp.

- Egg – 1

- Parmesan cheese – 2 tbsp.

- Dried oregano – ½ tsp.

- Almond flour – 1 cup

- Baking soda – ¼ tsp.

- Salt and ground black pepper to taste

- Coconut milk – ½ cup

- Cheddar cheese – 1 cup, grated

Method

1. In a bowl, mix flour with oregano, salt, pepper, parmesan cheese, and baking soda.

2. In another bowl, mix coconut milk with egg, olive oil, and mix well.

3. Combine the 2 mixtures and whisk.

4. Add cheddar cheese, stir, pour the mixture into a lined muffin tray, and place in an oven at 350F for 25 minutes.

5. Cool and serve.

Nutritional Facts Per Serving

- Calories: 204

- Fat: 19g

- Carb: 2.5g

- Protein: 7.6g

Turkey Breakfast

Prep Time: 10 minutes

Cook Time: 20 minutes

Serving: 1

Ingredients

- Avocado – 2 slices

- Salt and black pepper to taste

- Bacon – 2 slices, diced

- Turkey breast – 2 slices, cooked

- Coconut oil – 2 tbsp.

- Eggs – 2, whisked

Method

1. Heat a pan over medium heat.

2. Add bacon slices and brown all over.

3. Heat another pan with oil over medium heat.

4. Add eggs, salt, pepper, and scramble.

5. Divide turkey breast slices, scrambled eggs, bacon, and avocado slices on 2 plates and serve.

Nutritional Facts Per Serving

- Calories: 791

- Fat: 64.3g

- Carb: 8.8g

- Protein: 41.8g

Breakfast Hash

Prep Time: 10 minutes

Cook Time: 16 minutes

Serving: 2

Ingredients

- Coconut oil – 1 tbsp.

- Garlic – 2 cloves, peeled and minced

- Beef stock – ½ cup

- Salt and ground black pepper to taste

- Onion – 1, peeled and chopped

- Corned beef – 2 cups, chopped

- Radishes – 1 pound, cut into quarters

Method

1. Heat up a pan with oil.

2. Add onion and stir-fry for 4 minutes.

3. Add radishes, stir-fry for 5 minutes.

4. Add garlic, stir-fry for 1 minute.

5. Add beef, stock, salt, pepper, and stir-fry for 5 minutes.

6. Serve.

Nutritional Facts Per Serving

- Calories: 316

- Fat: 21.2g

- Carb: 3.8g

- Protein: 18g

Brussels Sprout Delight

Prep Time: 10 minutes

Cook Time: 12 minutes

Serving: 3

Ingredients

- Eggs – 3

- Salt and ground black pepper to taste

- Butter – 1 tbsp. melted

- Shallots – 2, peeled and minced

- Garlic – 2 cloves, peeled and minced

- Brussels sprouts – 12 ounces, sliced thin

- Bacon – 2 ounces, chopped

- Apple cider vinegar – 1 ½ tbsp.

Method

1. Heat a pan over medium heat.

2. Add bacon. Stir-fry until crispy. Transfer to a plate and set aside.

3. Heat the pan again over medium heat.

4. Add shallots and garlic. Stir-fry for 30 seconds.

5. Add Brussels sprouts, salt, pepper, and apple cider vinegar. Stir-fry for 5 minutes.

6. Return bacon to pan, stir, and cook for 5 minutes.

7. Add butter, stir, and make a hole in the center.

8. Crack eggs into the pan, and cook thoroughly.

9. Serve.

Nutritional Facts Per Serving

- Calories: 275

- Fat: 16.5g

- Carb: 7.2g

- Protein: 17.4g

Chia Pudding

Prep Time: 10 minutes

Cook Time: 30 minutes

Serving: 2

Ingredients

• Coffee – 2 tbsp.

• Water – 2 cups

• Chia seeds – 1/3 cup

• Swerve – 1 tbsp.

• Vanilla extract - 1 tbsp.

• Cocoa nibs – 2 tbsp.

• Coconut cream – 1/3 cup

Method

1. Heat a small pot with water over medium heat.

2. Bring to a boil, add coffee and simmer for 15 minutes. Strain into a bowl.

3. Add vanilla extract, coconut cream, swerve, cocoa nibs, and chia seeds. Mix well.

4. Keep in the refrigerator for 30 minutes.

5. Serve.

Nutritional Facts Per Serving

- Calories: 149

- Fat: 12.5g

- Carb: 8.8g

- Protein: 2g

Hemp Porridge

Prep Time: 3 minutes

Cook Time: 3 minutes

Serving: 1

Ingredients

• Chia seeds – 1 tbsp.

• Almond milk – 1 cup

• Flaxseeds – 2 tbsp.

• Hemp hearts – ½ cup

• Ground cinnamon – ½ tsp.

• Stevia - 1 tbsp.

• Vanilla extract – ¾ tsp.

• Almond flour – ¼ cup

• Hemp hearts – 1 tbsp. for serving

Method

1. In a pan, mix almond milk with ½ cup hemp hearts, chia seeds, stevia, flaxseeds, cinnamon, and vanilla extract. Mix well and heat over medium heat.

2. Cook for 2 minutes, and remove from the heat.

3. Add almond flour. Stir well and pour into a bowl.

4. Top with 1 tbsp. hemp hearts. Serve.

Nutritional Facts Per Serving

- Calories: 530

- Fat: 51g

- Carb: 2.7g

- Protein: 29.5g

Simple Breakfast Cereal

Prep Time: 10 minutes

Cook Time: 3 minutes

Serving: 2

Ingredients

- Coconut – ½ cup, shredded

- Butter – 4 tsp.

- Almond milk – 2 cups

- Stevia – 1 tbsp.

- Pinch of salt

- Macadamia nuts – 1/3 cup, chopped

- Walnuts – 1/3 cup, chopped

- Flaxseed – 1/3 cup

Method

1. Melt the butter in a pan.

2. Add coconut, milk, salt, macadamia nuts, walnuts, flaxseed, stevia, and stir well.

3. Cook for 3 minutes, stir again. Remove from heat and set aside for 10 minutes.

4. Serve.

Nutritional Facts Per Serving

- Calories: 588

- Fat: 48g

- Carb: 6.8g

- Protein: 16.5g

Egg Porridge

Prep Time: 10 minutes

Cook Time: 4 minutes

Serving: 2

Ingredients

- Eggs – 2
- Stevia – 1 tbsp.
- Heavy cream – 1/3 cup
- Butter – 2 tbsp. melted
- A pinch of ground cinnamon

Method

1. Mix the eggs with stevia and heavy cream. Whisk well.
2. Heat a pan with butter.
3. Add egg mixture and cook until done.
4. Transfer to 2 bowls.

5. Sprinkle with cinnamon and serve.

Nutritional Facts Per Serving

- Calories: 234

- Fat: 23.3g

- Carb: 1g

- Protein: 6.1g

Pancakes

Prep Time: 3 minutes

Cook Time: 12 minutes

Serving: 4

Ingredients

- Ground cinnamon – ½ tsp.

- Stevia – 1 tsp.

- Eggs – 2

- Olive oil cooking spray

- Cream cheese – 2 ounces

Method

1. In a blender, mix eggs with cream cheese, stevia, and cinnamon. Blend well.

2. Grease a pan with cooking spray and heat over medium-high heat.

3. Pour ¼ batter and spread well.

4. Cook for 2 minutes, flip and cook for 1 minute more.

5. Repeat with the rest of the batter.

6. Serve.

Nutritional Facts Per Serving

- Calories: 82

- Fat: 7.1g

- Carb: 1.3g

- Protein: 3.9g

Almond Pancakes

Prep Time: 10 minutes

Cook Time: 10 minutes

Serving: 12

Ingredients

- Eggs – 6

- A pinch of salt

- Coconut flour – ½ cup

- Stevia – ¼ cup

- Coconut – 1/3 cup, shredded

- Baking powder – ½ tsp.

- Almond milk – 1 cup

- Coconut oil – ¼ cup

- Almond extract – 1 tsp.

- Almonds – ¼ cup, toasted

- Cocoa powder – 2 ounces

- Olive oil cooking spray

Method

1. In a bowl, mix coconut flour with stevia, salt, baking powder, coconut, and stir. Add coconut oil, eggs, almond milk, almond extract, and mix well.

2. Add almonds, cocoa powder, and whisk again.

3. Heat a pan with cooking spray over medium heat.

4. Add 2 tbsp. batter, and spread into a circle.

5. Cook until golden, flip, cook again until done.

6. Repeat with the remaining batter and serve.

Nutritional Facts Per Serving

- Calories: 178

- Fat: 14.6g

- Carb: 9.8g

- Protein: 5.6g

French Toast

Prep Time: 5 minutes

Cook Time: 45 minutes

Serving: 18

Ingredients

- Whey protein – 1 cup

- Egg whites – 12

- Cream cheese – 4 ounces

  For the French toast

- Vanilla extract – 1 tsp.

- Coconut milk – ½ cup

- Eggs – 2

- Ground cinnamon – 1 tsp.

- Butter – ½ cup, melted

- Almond milk – ½ cup

- Swerve – ½ cup

Method

1. In a bowl, mix 12 egg whites with a mixer for a few minutes.

2. Add protein and stir gently. Add cream cheese and stir again.

3. Pour into 2 greased bread pans.

4. Place in an oven at 325F and bake for 45 minutes.

5. Cool and slice into 18 pieces.

6. In a bowl mix 2 eggs with vanilla extract, cinnamon, and coconut milk. Whisk. Dip bread slices in this mixture.

7. Heat a pan with coconut oil.

8. Add bread slices, and cook until golden on each side. Divide between plates.

9. Heat a pan with butter over high heat.

10.Add almond milk and heat through.

11.Add swerve, stir and remove from the heat.

12.Cool and drizzle for French toast slices.

13.Serve.

Nutritional Facts Per Serving

- Calories: 124

- Fat: 11g

- Carb: 5.3g

- Protein: 1.2g

Waffles

Prep Time: 10 minutes

Cook Time: 20 minutes

Serving: 5

Ingredients

- Eggs – 5, separated

- Almond milk – 3 tbsp.

- Baking powder – 1 tsp.

- Stevia – 3 tbsp.

- Coconut flour – 4 tbsp.

- Vanilla extract – 2 tsp.

- Butter – 4 ounces, melted

Method

1. In a bowl, whisk egg whites using a mixer.

2. In another bowl, mix flour with stevia, baking powder, and egg yolks, and whisk well.

3. Add butter, vanilla extract, milk, and stir well. Add egg whites and stir.

4. Pour some of the mixtures into a waffle maker and cook until golden.

5. Repeat with the rest of the batter and serve.

Nutritional Facts Per Serving

- Calories: 255

- Fat: 25g

- Carb: 1.5g

- Protein: 6.1g

Chapter 6: Lunch Recipes

Zucchini Boats

Prep Time: 10 minutes

Cook Time: 35 minutes

Serving: 1

Ingredients

- Large zucchinis – 2

- Butter – 2 tbsp.

- Shredded cheddar cheese – 3 oz.

- Broccoli – 1 cup

- Shredded rotisserie chicken – 6 oz.

- Green onion – 1 stalk

- Sour cream – 2 tbsp.

- Salt and pepper

Method

1. Cut the zucchini in half lengthwise, scooping out the core until you are left with a boat shape.

2. Into each zucchini, pour a little melted butter, season, and place into the oven at 400F. Bake for 18 minutes.

3. In a bowl, combine the broccoli, chicken and sour cream.

4. Place the chicken mixture inside the hollowed zucchinis.

5. Top with cheddar cheese and bake for 10 to 15 minutes more.

6. Serve.

Nutritional Facts Per Serving

• Calories: 480

• Fat: 35g

• Carb: 5g

• Protein: 28g

Chicken Sandwich

Prep Time: 10 minutes

Cook Time: 25 minutes

Serving: 2

Ingredients for the bread

- Eggs – 3

- Cream cheese – 3 oz.

- Cream of tartar – 1/8 tsp.

- Salt and garlic powder

For the filling

- Mayonnaise – 1 tbsp.

- Sriracha – 1 tsp.

- Bacon – 2 slices

- Chicken – 3 oz.

- Pepper jack cheese – 2 slices

- Grape tomatoes – 2

- Avocado – ¼

Method

1. Separate the eggs into different bowls. In the bowl with the egg whites, add cream of tartar, salt, and beat until stiff peaks form.

2. In another bowl, beat the egg yolks with cream cheese.

3. Incorporate the mixture into the egg white mixture and combine carefully.

4. Place the batter on a parchment paper and form little square shapes that look like bread slices.

5. Sprinkle garlic powder on top and bake at 300F for 25 minutes.

6. Meanwhile, cook the chicken and bacon in a pan. Season to taste.

7. When the bread is done, remove from the oven and cool.

8. Make a sandwich with the cooked chicken and bacon, adding the sriracha, mayo, tomatoes, cheese and mashed avocado to taste.

Nutritional Facts Per Serving

- Calories: 360

- Fat: 28g

- Carb: 3g

- Protein: 22g

Tuna Bites with Avocado

Prep Time: 5 minutes

Cook Time: 5 to 7 minutes

Serving: 8

Ingredients

- Drained canned tuna – 10 oz.

- Mayo – ¼ cup

- Avocado – 1

- Parmesan cheese – ¼ cup

- Almond flour – 1/3 cup

- Garlic powder – ½ tsp.

- Onion powder – ¼ tsp.

- Coconut oil – ½ cup

- Salt and pepper

Method

1. Except for the coconut oil, mix all the ingredients in a bowl. Form little balls and cover with almond flour.

2. Fry them in a pan with melted coconut oil until they seem browned on all sides.

3. Serve with salad.

Nutritional Facts Per Serving

- Calories: 137

- Fat: 12g

- Carb: 10g

- Protein: 6g

Sausage and Pepper Soup

Prep Time: 5 minutes

Cook Time: 50 minutes

Serving: 6

Ingredients

• Pork sausage – 30 oz.

• Olive oil – 1 tbsp.

• Raw spinach – 10 oz.

• Medium green bell pepper – 1

• Tomatoes with jalapenos – 1 can

• Beef stock – 4 cups

• Onion powder – 1 tbsp.

• Chili powder – 1 tbsp.

• Garlic powder – 1 tsp.

• Italian seasoning – 1 tsp.

• Salt

Method

1. Heat the olive oil in a pot. Add sausage and stir-fry it.

2. Chop the green pepper and add to the pot. Mix well.

3. Season with salt and pepper and add the tomatoes and jalapenos. Mix.

4. Add the spinach on top and cover the pot.

5. When it is wilted, incorporate spices and broth and combine.

6. Cover the pot again and cook for 30 minutes.

7. Remove the lid and let the soup simmer for 10 minutes.

8. Serve.

Nutritional Facts Per Serving

- Calories: 525

- Fat: 45g

- Carb: 4g

- Protein: 28g

Chicken Nuggets

Prep Time: 5 minutes

Cook Time: 7 to 10 minutes

Serving: 4

Ingredients

• Chicken breast – 1, precooked

• Grated parmesan – ½ ounce

• Almond flour – 2 tbsp.

• Baking powder – ½ tsp.

• Egg – 1

• Water – 1 tbsp.

Method

1. Cut the chicken breast into slices and then into bite-size pieces. Set aside.

2. Combine the baking powder, almond flour, parmesan, and water. Stir.

3. Cover the chicken pieces in the batter, and place into the hot oil.

4. Cook and serve.

Nutritional Facts Per Serving

- Calories: 165

- Fat: 9g

- Carb: 3g

- Protein: 25g

Cauliflower Rice with Chicken

Prep Time: 5 minutes

Cook Time: 25 minutes

Serving: 6

Ingredients

• Chicken breasts – 4

• Curry paste – 1 packet

• Water – 1 cup

• Ghee – 3 tbsp.

• Heavy cream – ½ cup

• Cauliflower – 1 head, chopped into florets

Method

1. In a pan, melt the ghee, add the curry and stir.

2. Add the water, and simmer for 5 minutes.

3. Add the chicken, cover, and keep cooking for 20 minutes.

4. Add the cream and cook for 5 minutes more.

5. Meanwhile, sauté the florets in a frying pan with a little butter.

6. Lower the heat and cover with a lid.

7. Simmer for 5 to 8 minutes.

8. Serve along with the chicken curry.

Nutritional Facts Per Serving

- Calories: 350

- Fat: 16g

- Carb: 10g

- Protein: 40g

Chicken and Bacon Casserole

Prep Time: 5 minutes

Cook Time: 1 hour

Serving: 12

Ingredients

• Chicken thighs – 12

• Small onion – 1, chopped

• Celery stalks – 4

• Sausage – 24 oz.

• Sliced mushrooms – 16 oz.

• Frozen cauliflower – 16 oz. defrosted and florets cut into smaller pieces

• Bacon – 7 slices

• Shredded cheddar cheese – 8 oz.

• Cream cheese – 16 oz. softened

• Paprika

Method

1. Cook the bacon in the oven at 400F for 15 minutes.

2. Meanwhile, dice the chicken and cook in a frying pan. Remove from the pan.

3. Brown the sausage. Once it is done, place it on the chicken bowl.

4. Chop the onion and celery. Cook them in the remaining sausage grease until translucent.

5. In a bowl, add all the ingredients and mix well. Add the cream cheese and mix well.

6. In a pan, place the mixture and sprinkle the paprika.

7. Bake at 350F for 30 minutes, covered with foil.

8. Uncover and cook for 10 minutes more.

Nutritional Facts Per Serving

- Calories: 600

- Fat: 41g

- Carb: 6g

- Protein: 53g

Mexican Casserole

Prep Time: 10 minutes

Cook Time: 1 hour

Serving: 12

Ingredients

• Green pepper – 1, chopped

• Onion – 1, chopped

• Drained spinach – 20 oz.

• Ground pork – 2 lb.

• Drained diced tomatoes with green chilies – 2 cans

• Sour cream – 10 tbsp.

• Mozzarella cheese – 8 oz. shredded

• Cream cheese – 16 oz.

• Taco seasoning – 4 tsp.

• Jalapenos, sliced

Method

1. Cook the chopped pepper and onion until translucent. Place in a bowl.

2. Cook the spinach until wilted in the pan with a little oil. Add to the bowl.

3. Cook the ground pork until browned. Season with taco seasoning.

4. Add the diced tomato to the bowl, and incorporate the sour cream, mozzarella, and cream cheese.

5. Pour the mixture into a baking dish, and bake at 350F for 40 minutes.

Nutritional Facts Per Serving

- Calories: 400

- Fat: 30g

- Carb: 10g

- Protein: 25g

Almond Pizza

Prep Time: 5 minutes

Cook Time: 12 minutes

Serving: 4

Ingredients

- Almond meal – ¾ cup

- Baking powder – 1 ½ tsp.

- Granulated sweetener – 1 ½ tsp.

- Oregano – ½ tsp.

- Thyme – ¼ tsp.

- Garlic powder – ½ tsp.

- Eggs – 2

- Butter – 5 tbsp.

- Alfredo sauce – ½ cup

- Cheddar cheese – 4 oz.

Method

1. Mix the dry ingredients together in a bowl.

2. Add the eggs to the dry mixture.

3. Melt the butter and incorporate.

4. On a greased pizza pan, spread the crust and pre-cook at 350F for 7 minutes.

5. Remove from the oven and spread the Alfredo sauce and cheddar cheese on top.

6. Cook for 5 minutes more and serve.

Nutritional Facts Per Serving

• Calories: 460

• Fat: 45g

• Carb: 5g

• Protein: 15g

Chicken Thighs

Prep Time: 5 minutes

Cook Time: 20 minutes

Serving: 6

Ingredients

• Boneless, skinless chicken thighs - 16

• Water – 2 cups

• Cheddar cheese – 8 oz. shredded

• Spinach – 24 oz.

• Salt and pepper

• Garlic powder

Method

1. Bake the chicken thighs in a covered pan with 2 cups of water at 350F for 20 minutes. Remove and cool.

2. Break the chicken into pieces, adding the spinach, cheese, and seasonings.

3. Serve.

Nutritional Facts Per Serving

- Calories: 390

- Fat: 25g

- Carb: 4g

- Protein: 47g

Grilled Cheese Sandwich

Prep Time: 5 minutes

Cook Time: 5 to 7 minutes

Serving: 1

Ingredients

- Eggs – 2

- Almond flour – 2 tbsp.

- Psyllium husk powder – 1 ½ tbsp.

- Baking powder – ½ tsp.

- Soft butter – 2 tbsp.

- Cheddar cheese – 2 oz.

- Butter – 1 tbsp.

Method

1. Mix the eggs, psyllium husk powder, almond flour, baking powder, and butter to make the bun.

2. Place the mixture into a square container and let it sit to level itself.

3. Microwave for 90 seconds.

4. When it is cooked, remove and slice in half.

5. Place the cheese between the bun halves, and fry in a pan with melted butter.

6. Serve.

Nutritional Facts Per Serving

- Calories: 794

- Fat: 72g

- Carb: 5g

- Protein: 30g

Crisp Pizza

Prep Time: 5 minutes

Cook Time: 30 minutes

Serving: 12

Ingredients

- Cream cheese – 8 oz. package

- Parmesan cheese – ¼ cup, grated

- Eggs – 2

- Garlic powder – 1 tsp.

- Ground beef – ½ lb.

- Chorizo sausage – 1

- Cumin - ½ tsp.

- Basil – ¼ tsp.

- Italian seasoning – ½ tsp.

- Turmeric – ¼ tsp.

- Salt and pepper

Method

1. Mix cream cheese, eggs, parmesan cheese, pepper, and garlic with a hand blender.

2. Grease a baking pan with butter.

3. Spread the dough mixture evenly inside.

4. Cook for 12 to 15 minutes in the oven at 375F.

5. Cook the meat in a frying pan and add the spices: basil, cumin, Italian seasoning, and turmeric.

6. Once the pizza crust is done, cool for 10 minutes.

7. Cover with the tomato sauce and some cheese.

8. Bake for 10 minutes more. When the cheese starts to melt, add the meat.

9. Broil for 5 minutes more.

10. Cool, slice and serve.

Nutritional Facts Per Serving

- Calories: 145

- Fat: 12g

- Carb: 1g

- Protein: 9g

Meatballs with Bacon and Cheese

Prep Time: 5 minutes

Cook Time: 15 minutes

Serving: 5

Ingredients

- Ground beef – 1 ½ lb.

- Pork rinds – ¾ cup, crushed to powder

- Salt – ¾ tsp.

- Pepper – ¾ tsp.

- Cumin – ¾ tsp.

- Garlic powder – ¾ tsp.

- Cheddar cheese – ¾ cup

- Bacon – 4 slices

- Egg – 1

Method

1. Mix the pork rinds, ground beef, salt, pepper, cumin, and garlic powder. Add the cheese and mix well.

2. Cut the bacon into small pieces and fry them in the hot pan until cooked. Cool.

3. Add the bacon to the meat and combine well.

4. Form the meatballs.

5. Cook the meatballs in a pan, browning them on all sides, then cover with a lid for 10 minutes.

6. When finished, let them sit for 5 minutes.

7. Top with the sauce of your choice and serve.

Nutritional Facts Per Serving

- Calories: 450

- Fat: 26g

- Carb: 3g

- Protein: 50g

Sausage & Cabbage Skillet Melt

Prep Time: 5 minutes

Cook Time: 16 minutes

Serving: 4

Ingredients

- Spicy Italian chicken sausages – 4

- Green cabbage – 1 ½ cups, shredded

- Purple cabbage – 1 ½ cups, shredded

- Onion -1/2 cup, diced

- Coconut oil – 2 tsp.

- Colby jack cheese – 2 slices

- Fresh cilantro – 2 tsp. chopped

Method

1. Melt the coconut oil, and fry the onion and cabbage in a skillet.

2. Cook for 8 minutes on medium heat.

3. Add the sausage, and stir to mix it into the vegetables. Cook for 8 minutes more.

4. Add the cheese on top and cover.

5. Turn off the heat and wait while the cheese melts into the vegetables.

6. Serve.

Nutritional Facts Per Serving

- Calories: 233

- Fat: 15g

- Carb: 5g

- Protein: 20g

Kung Pao Chicken

Prep Time: 5 minutes

Cook Time: 15 minutes

Serving: 3

Ingredients for the chicken

• Chicken thighs – 2 medium

• Ground ginger – 1 tsp.

• Peanuts – ¼ cup

• Green pepper – ½

• De-seeded red bird's eye chilies – 4

• Spring onions – 2 large

• Salt and pepper

For the sauce

• Liquid aminos - 1 tbsp.

• Chili garlic paste – 2 tbsp.

- Rice wine vinegar – 2 tsp.

- No sugar added ketchup – 1 tbsp.

- Maple extract – ½ tsp.

- Sesame oil – 2 tsp.

- Liquid stevia – 10 drops

Method

1. Cut the chicken into small pieces and season with salt, pepper, and ginger.

2. Cook the chicken in a pan for 10 minutes.

3. Make the sauce by combining all the sauce ingredients.

4. Chop the vegetables and chilies.

5. When the chicken is done, add all the ingredients and cook for 3 to 4 minutes longer.

6. Add the sauce and let it boil until reduced.

7. Serve.

Nutritional Facts Per Serving

- Calories: 360

- Fat: 27.5g

- Carb: 3g

- Protein: 22g

Chapter 7: Side Dish Recipes

Simple Kimchi

Prep Time: 1 hour 10 minutes

Cook Time: 0 minutes

Serving: 6

Ingredients

- Salt – 3 tbsp.

- Napa cabbage - 1 pound, chopped

- Butternut squash – 3 oz. julienned

- Daikon radish – ½ cup

- Green onion stalks – 3, chopped

- Fish sauce – 1 tbsp.

- Chili flakes – 3 tbsp.

- Garlic – 3 cloves, peeled and minced

- Sesame oil - 1 tbsp.

- Fresh ginger – ½ inch, peeled and grated

Method

1. In a bowl, mix cabbage with salt, and massage well for 10 minutes. Cover and set aside for 1 hour.

2. In a bowl, mix the chili flakes with garlic, fish sauce, sesame oil, ginger, and stir well.

3. Drain cabbage well, rinse under cold water and transfer to a bowl.

4. Add green onions, squash, radish, and chili paste. Mix.

5. Leave in a dark and cold place for 2 days before serving.

Nutritional Facts Per Serving

- Calories: 43

- Fat: 2.5g

- Carb: 4.9g

- Protein: 1.6g

Oven-fried Green Beans

Prep Time: 10 minutes

Cook Time: 10 minutes

Serving: 4

Ingredients

- Parmesan cheese – 2/3 cup, grated

- Egg – 1

- Green beans – 12 ounces

- Salt and ground black pepper to taste

- Garlic powder – ½ tsp.

- Paprika – ¼ tsp.

Method

1. In a bowl, mix Parmesan cheese with salt, pepper, garlic powder, and paprika. In another bowl, whisk the egg with salt and pepper.

2. Coat the green beans in egg, and then in the Parmesan mixture.

3. Place green beans on a lined baking sheet, place in an oven at 400F for 10 minutes.

4. Serve hot.

Nutritional Facts Per Serving

• Calories: 66

• Fat: 2.7g

• Carb: 6.7g

• Protein: 5.3g

Cauliflower Mash

Prep Time: 10 minutes

Cook Time: 10 minutes

Serving: 2

Ingredients

- Sour cream – ¼ cup

- Small cauliflower head – 1, separated into florets

- Salt and ground black pepper to taste

- Feta cheese – 2 tbsp. crumbled

- Black olives – 2 tbsp. pitted and sliced

Method

1. Put water in a saucepan, add some salt, bring to a boil over medium heat.

2. Add the florets, and cook for 10 minutes. Remove from heat and drain.

3. Return cauliflower to the saucepan, add salt, black pepper, and sour cream, and blend with a hand mixer.

4. Add black olives and feta cheese.

5. Stir and serve.

Nutritional Facts Per Serving

- Calories: 129

- Fat: 9.1g

- Carb: 9.2g

- Protein: 4.9g

Portobello Mushrooms

Prep Time: 10 minutes

Cook Time: 10 minutes

Serving: 4

Ingredients

- Portobello mushrooms – 12 ounces, sliced

- Salt and black pepper to taste

- Dried basil – ½ tsp.

- Olive oil – 2 tbsp.

- Tarragon – ½ tsp. dried

- Dried rosemary – ½ tsp.

- Dried thyme – ½ tsp.

- Balsamic vinegar – 2 tbsp.

Method

1. In a bowl, mix the oil with vinegar, salt, pepper, rosemary, tarragon, thyme, and basil. Whisk to mix.

2. Add mushroom slices, toss to coat well. Place them on a preheated grill over medium-high heat.

3. Cook for 5 minutes on both sides.

4. Serve.

Nutritional Facts Per Serving

- Calories: 85

- Fat: 7g

- Carb: 2.5g

- Protein: 2.5g

Pesto

Prep Time: 10 minutes

Cook Time: 0 minutes

Serving: 4

Ingredients

- Olive oil – ½ cup

- Basil – 2 cups

- Pine nuts – 1/3 cup

- Parmesan cheese – 1/3 cup, grated

- Garlic – 2 cloves, peeled and chopped

- Salt and ground black pepper to taste

Method

1. Put basil in a food processor, add pine nuts and garlic, and blend well.

2. Add the salt, Parmesan cheese, pepper, and the oil gradually, and blend again until you obtain a paste.

3. Serve with chicken or vegetables.

Nutritional Facts Per Serving

- Calories: 320

- Fat: 34.5g

- Carb: 2.6g

- Protein: 4.3g

Brussels Sprouts and Bacon

Prep Time: 10 minutes

Cook Time: 30 minutes

Serving: 4

Ingredients

- Bacon strips – 8, chopped

- Brussels sprouts – 1 pound, trimmed and halved

- Salt and ground black pepper to taste

- A pinch of cumin

- A pinch of red pepper, crushed

- Extra virgin olive oil – 2 tbsp.

Method

1. In a bowl, mix Brussels sprouts with salt, pepper, oil, red pepper, and cumin. Toss to coat.

2. Spread Brussels sprouts on a lined baking sheet.

3. Place in an oven at 375F and bake for 30 minutes.

4. Heat a pan over medium heat, add bacon pieces, and cook them until crispy.

5. Divide baked Brussels sprouts on plates.

6. Top with bacon and serve.

Nutritional Facts Per Serving

• Calories: 159

• Fat: 11.9g

• Carb: 8.3g

• Protein: 5.9g

Avocado Fries

Prep Time: 10 minutes

Cook Time: 5 minutes

Serving: 3

Ingredients

- Avocados – 3, pitted, peeled, halved, and sliced

- Olive oil – 1 ½ cups

- Almond meal – 1 ½ cups

- A pinch of cayenne pepper

- Salt and ground black pepper to taste

Method

1. In a bowl, mix the almond meal with salt, pepper, cayenne, and stir.

2. In another bowl, whisk eggs with a pinch of salt and pepper.

3. Coat the avocado pieces in egg, and then in almond meal mixture.

4. Heat a pan with oil over medium-high heat.

5. Add avocado fries, and cook them until they are golden.

6. Transfer to paper towels, and drain grease.

7. Serve.

Nutritional Facts Per Serving

- Calories: 480

- Fat: 72g

- Carb: 7.5g

- Protein: 13.9g

Mushroom and Spinach

Prep Time: 10 minutes

Cook Time: 10 minutes

Serving: 4

Ingredients

- Spinach leaves – 10 ounces, chopped

- Salt and ground black pepper to taste

- Mushrooms – 14 ounces, chopped

- Garlic – 2 cloves, peeled and minced

- Fresh parsley – ½ cup, chopped

- Onion -1, peeled and chopped

- Olive oil - 4 tbsp.

- Balsamic vinegar – 2 tbsp.

Method

1. Heat a pan with oil over medium-high heat.

2. Add onion, garlic, and stir-fry for 4 minutes.

3. Add mushrooms, and stir-fry for 3 minutes.

4. Add spinach, and stir-fry for 3 minutes.

5. Add salt, vinegar, pepper, and stir-fry for 1 minute.

6. Add parsley, stir, and divide between plates.

7. Serve.

Nutritional Facts Per Serving

- Calories: 175

- Fat: 14.7g

- Carb: 8.2g

- Protein: 5.8g

Okra and Tomatoes

Prep Time: 10 minutes

Cook Time: 10 minutes

Serving: 6

Ingredients

• Canned stewed tomatoes – 14 ounces, cored and chopped

• Salt and ground black pepper to taste

• Celery stalks – 2, chopped

• Onion – 1, peeled and chopped

• Okra – 1 pound, trimmed and sliced

• Bacon slices – 2, chopped

• Small green bell pepper – 1, seeded and chopped

Method

1. Heat a pan over medium heat.

2. Add bacon, stir, and brown for a few minutes. Transfer to paper towels and set aside.

3. Heat the pan again and add bell pepper, okra, onion, and celery. Stir and cook for 2 minutes.

4. Add salt, pepper, and tomatoes. Stir-fry for 3 minutes.

5. Divide between plates.

6. Garnish with crispy bacon and serve.

Nutritional Facts Per Serving

• Calories: 91

• Fat: 3g

• Carb: 5g

• Protein: 4.7g

Collard Greens with Turkey

Prep Time: 10 minutes

Cook Time: 2 hour and 15 minutes

Serving: 10

Ingredients

- Collard greens – 5 bunches, chopped

- Salt and ground black pepper to taste

- Red pepper flakes - 1 tbsp.

- Chicken stock – 5 cups

- Turkey – 1 leg

- Garlic – 2 tbsp. minced

- Olive oil – ¼ cup

Method

1. Heat a pot with oil over medium heat.

2. Add garlic, stir, and cook for 1 minute.

3. Add stock, salt, pepper, turkey leg, stir, cover, and simmer for 30 minutes.

4. Add collard greens, cover pot again, and cook for 45 minutes.

5. Reduce heat to medium, add more salt and pepper, stir and cook for 1 hour.

6. Drain the greens, chop up the turkey.

7. Mix everything with the red pepper flakes.

8. Stir and divide between plates.

9. Serve.

Nutritional Facts Per Serving

• Calories: 171

• Fat: 10.9g

• Carb: 2.2g

• Protein: 16.1g

Eggplant and Tomatoes

Prep Time: 10 minutes

Cook Time: 15 minutes

Serving: 4

Ingredients

- Tomato – 1, sliced

- Eggplant – 1, sliced into thin rounds

- Salt and ground black pepper to taste

- Parmesan cheese – ¼ cup, to taste

- A drizzle of olive oil

Method

1. Place eggplant slices on a lined baking dish.

2. Drizzle some oil, and sprinkle half of the Parmesan.

3. Top eggplant slices with tomato ones, season with salt and pepper. Sprinkle the rest of the cheese over them.

4. Place in an oven at 400F and bake for 15 minutes.

5. Serve.

Nutritional Facts Per Serving

- Calories: 73

- Fat: 4.5g

- Carb: 7.2g

- Protein: 2.4g

Broccoli with Lemon Almond Butter

Prep Time: 10 minutes

Cook Time: 10 minutes

Serving: 4

Ingredients

- Broccoli – 1 head, separated into florets

- Salt and ground black pepper to taste

- Almonds – ¼ cup, blanched

- Lemon zest – 1 tsp.

- Coconut butter – ¼ cup, melted

- Lemon juice – 2 tbsp.

Method

1. Put water in a saucepan, add the salt, and bring to a boil over medium-high heat.

2. Place broccoli florets in a steamer basket. Place into saucepan, cover, and steam for 8 minutes. Drain and transfer to a bowl.

3. Heat a pan with the coconut butter over medium heat; add the lemon juice, lemon zest, and almonds. Stir, and take off the heat.

4. Add the broccoli, toss to coat, divide onto plates and serve.

Nutritional Facts Per Serving

• Calories: 168

• Fat: 12.4g

• Carb: 12.6g

• Protein: 5.5g

Sautéed Broccoli

Prep Time: 10 minutes

Cook Time: 22 minutes

Serving: 4

Ingredients

- Olive oil – 5 tbsp.

- Garlic – 1 clove, peeled and minced

- Broccoli florets – 1 pound

- Parmesan cheese – 1 tbsp. grated

- Salt and ground black pepper to taste

Method

1. Put water in a saucepan, add salt, bring to a boil over medium heat.

2. Add broccoli, cook for 5 minutes, then drain.

3. Heat a pan with oil over medium-high heat. Add garlic, stir and cook for 2 minutes.

4. Add broccoli and cook for 15 minutes. Take off heat.

5. Sprinkle Parmesan cheese.

6. Serve.

Nutritional Facts Per Serving

• Calories: 195

• Fat: 18.2g

• Carb: 7.8g

• Protein: 3.8g

Greek Side Salad

Prep Time: 10 minutes

Cook Time: 7 minutes

Serving: 6

Ingredients

- Mushrooms – ½ pounds, sliced

- Extra virgin olive oil – 1 tbsp.

- Garlic – 3 cloves, peeled and minced

- Dried basil – 1 tsp.

- Salt and ground black pepper to taste

- Tomato – 1, cored and diced

- Lemon juice – 3 tbsp.

- Water – ½ cup

- Coriander – 1 tbsp. chopped

Method

1. Heat a pan with oil over medium heat.

2. Add mushrooms and stir-fry for 3 minutes.

3. Add garlic and basil and stir-fry for 1 minute.

4. Add salt, pepper, water, tomato, and lemon juice. Stir and cook for a few minutes.

5. Remove from heat and cool.

6. Sprinkle with coriander and serve.

Nutritional Facts Per Serving

- Calories: 34

- Fat: 2.5g

- Carb: 2.3g

- Protein: 1.4g

Summer Side Salad

Prep Time: 10 minutes

Cook Time: 5 minutes

Serving: 6

Ingredients

- Extra virgin olive oil – ½ cup

- Cucumber – 1, chopped

- Colored cherry tomatoes – 4 cups, cut into half

- Salt and ground black pepper to taste

- Onion – 1, chopped

- Balsamic vinegar – 3 tbsp.

- Garlic – 1 clove, peeled and minced

- Fresh basil – 1 bunch, chopped

Method

1. In a bowl, mix vinegar with salt, pepper, and olive oil and whisk.

2. In a salad bowl, mix the cucumber with tomatoes, garlic, and onion.

3. Add vinegar dressing, toss to coat.

4. Sprinkle the basil. Add more salt and pepper if needed. Toss to coat.

5. Serve.

Nutritional Facts Per Serving

• Calories: 171

• Fat: 17g

• Carb: 5.8g

• Protein: 1.3g

Chapter 8: Snack and Appetizer Recipes

Marinated Eggs

Prep Time: 2 hours and 10 minutes

Cook Time: 7 minutes

Serving: 4

Ingredients

- Eggs – 6

- Water – 1 ¼ cups

- Unsweetened rice vinegar – ¼ cup

- Coconut aminos – 2 tbsp.

- Salt and ground black pepper to taste

- Garlic – 2 cloves, peeled and minced

- Stevia – 1 tsp.

- Cream cheese – 4 ounces

- Fresh chives – 1 tbsp. chopped

Method

1. Put eggs in a pot, add water to cover, bring to a boil over medium heat, cover, and cook for 7 minutes.

2. Rinse eggs with cold water, and set them aside to cool down.

3. In a bowl, mix 1-cup water with vinegar, coconut aminos, stevia, garlic, and whisk.

4. Put eggs in this mixture, cover with a kitchen towel, and set aside for 2 hours, rotating them from time to time.

5. Peel eggs, cut in half and put the egg yolks in a bowl.

6. Add remaining water, cream cheese, chives, salt, and pepper and stir well.

7. Stuff egg whites with mixture and serve.

Nutritional Facts Per Serving

- Calories: 201

- Fat: 16.5g

- Carb: 2.8g

- Protein: 10.6g

Onion and Cauliflower Dip

Prep Time: 2 hours

Cook Time: 30 minutes

Serving: 24

Ingredients

- Chicken stock – 1 ½ cups

- Cauliflower head – 1, separated into florets

- Mayonnaise – ¼ cup

- Onion – ½ cup, peeled and chopped

- Cream cheese – ¾ cup

- Chili powder – ½ tsp.

- Cumin – ½ tsp.

- Garlic powder – ½ tsp.

- Salt and ground black pepper to taste

Method

1. Put the stock in a saucepan, add the cauliflower and onion. Heat over medium heat, and cook for 30 minutes.

2. Add salt, pepper, chili powder, cumin, and garlic powder, and stir.

3. Add cream cheese, and stir a bit until it melts.

4. Blend with a hand mixer and mix with the mayonnaise.

5. Transfer to a bowl, and keep in the refrigerator for 2 hours before serving.

Nutritional Facts Per Serving

• Calories: 39

• Fat: 3.4g

• Carb: 1.6g

• Protein: 1g

Pesto Crackers

Prep Time: 10 minutes

Cook Time: 17 minutes

Serving: 6

Ingredients

- Baking powder – ½ tsp.

- Salt and ground black pepper to taste

- Almond flour – 1 ¼ cups

- Dried basil – ¼ tsp.

- Garlic – 1 clove, peeled and minced

- Basil pesto – 2 tbsp.

- A pinch of cayenne pepper

- Butter – 3 tbsp.

Method

1. In a bowl, mix salt, pepper, baking powder, and almond flour.

2. Add cayenne, garlic, and basil, and stir. Add pesto and whisk.

3. Add butter and mix the dough with your fingers.

4. Spread dough on a lined baking sheet.

5. Place in an oven at 325F and bake for 17 minutes.

6. Set aside to cool down, cut the crackers and serve.

Nutritional Facts Per Serving

• Calories: 154

• Fat: 14.9g

• Carb: 4.6g

• Protein: 4.2g

Pumpkin Muffins

Prep Time: 10 minutes

Cook Time: 15 minutes

Serving: 18

Ingredients

- Sunflower seed butter – ¼ cup

- Pumpkin puree – ¾ cup

- Flaxseed meal – 2 tbsp.

- Coconut flour – ¼ cup

- Erythritol – ½ cup

- Ground nutmeg – ½ tsp.

- Ground cinnamon – 1 tsp.

- Baking soda – ½ tsp.

- Egg – 1

- Baking powder – ½ tsp.

- A pinch of salt

Method

1. In a bowl, mix pumpkin puree, butter, and egg and blend well.

2. Add flaxseed meal, coconut flour, erythritol, baking soda, baking powder, nutmeg, cinnamon, and pinch of salt and stir well.

3. Spoon into a greased muffin pan, place in an oven at 350F and bake for 15 minutes.

4. Cool and serve.

Nutritional Facts Per Serving

- Calories: 42

- Fat: 2.6g

- Carb: 4.6g

- Protein: 1.6g

Tortilla Chips

Prep Time: 10 minutes

Cook Time: 14 minutes

Serving: 6

Ingredients for the tortillas

- Olive oil – 2 tsp.

- Flaxseed meal – 1 cup

- Psyllium husk powder – 2 tbsp.

- Xanthan gum – ¼ tsp.

- Water – 1 cup

- Curry powder – ½ tsp.

- Coconut flour – 3 tsp.

For the chips

- Flaxseed tortillas – 6

- Salt and ground black pepper to taste

- Olive oil – 3 tbsp.

- Fresh tomato paste for serving

• Sour cream for serving

Method

1. In a bowl, mix flaxseed meal with olive oil, psyllium powder, xanthan gum, water, curry powder, and mix until you get a dough.

2. Spread coconut flour on a work surface.

3. Divide dough into 6 pieces. Place each piece onto the work surface and roll into a circle. Cut each into 6 pieces.

4. Heat a pan with olive oil and add the tortilla chips. Cook for a few minutes on each side, and transfer to paper towels.

5. Put tortilla chips in a bowl, season with salt and pepper and serve with some fresh tomato paste and sour cream on the side.

Nutritional Facts Per Serving

• Calories: 335

• Fat: 18.8g

• Carb: 5.4g

• Protein: 8.6g

Jalapeno Balls

Prep Time: 10 minutes

Cook Time: 10 minutes

Serving: 3

Ingredients

- Bacon slices – 3
- Cream cheese – 3 ounces
- Onion powder – ¼ tsp.
- Salt and ground black pepper to taste
- Jalapeno pepper – 1, chopped
- Dried parsley – ½ tsp.
- Garlic powder – ¼ tsp.

Method

1. Heat a pan over medium heat.

2. Add bacon and cook until crispy. Transfer to paper towels and drain grease. Crumble.

3. Reserve bacon fat from the pan.

4. In a bowl, mix cream cheese with the onion powder, jalapeno pepper, garlic powder, parsley, salt, pepper, and stir well.

5. Add crumbled bacon and bacon fat. Stir gently.

6. Shape balls from this mixture and serve.

Nutritional Facts Per Serving

- Calories: 205

- Fat: 17.9g

- Carb: 1.6g

- Protein: 9.3g

Pepperoni Bombs

Prep Time: 10 minutes

Cook Time: 0 minutes

Serving: 6

Ingredients

- Black olives- 8, pitted and chopped

- Salt and ground black pepper to taste

- Sundried tomato pesto - 2 tbsp.

- Pepperoni slices – 14, chopped

- Cream cheese – 4 ounces

- Fresh basil – 1 tbsp. chopped

Method

1. In a bowl, mix cream cheese with salt, pepper, basil, pepperoni, sundried tomato pesto and black olives, and stir.

2. Shape balls from the mixture, arrange on a platter and serve.

Nutritional Facts Per Serving

- Calories: 140

- Fat: 6g

- Carb: 1.2g

- Protein: 4.5g

Cheeseburger Muffins

Prep Time: 10 minutes

Cook Time: 30 minutes

Serving: 9

Ingredients

- Flaxseed meal – ½ cup

- Almond flour – ½ cup

- Salt and ground black pepper to taste

- Eggs – 2

- Baking powder – 1 tsp.

- Sour cream – ¼ cups

For the filling

- Onion powder – ½ tsp.

- Ground beef – 16 ounces

- Salt and ground black pepper to taste

- Tomato paste – 2 tbsp. no sugar added

- Garlic powder – ½ tsp.

- Cheddar cheese – ½ cup, grated

- Mustard – 2 tbsp.

Method

1. In a bowl, mix almond flour with flaxseed meal, salt, pepper and baking powder, and whisk. Add eggs and sour cream and stir well.

2. Divide into a greased muffin pan and press well using your fingers.

3. Heat a pan over medium heat. Add beef, stir, and brown for a few minutes.

4. Add salt, pepper, onion powder, garlic powder, tomato paste, and stir well.

5. Cook for 5 minutes and remove from the heat.

6. Fill the cupcakes' crust with this mixture, place in the oven at 350F, and bake for 15 minutes.

7. Spread cheese on top, place in an oven again and bake for 5 minutes.

8. Serve.

Nutritional Facts Per Serving

- Calories: 203

- Fat: 9g

- Carb: 4.4g

- Protein: 20.5g

Pizza Dip

Prep Time: 10 minutes

Cook Time: 20 minutes

Serving: 4

Ingredients

- Cream cheese – 4 ounces, softened

- Mozzarella cheese – ½ cup

- Sour cream – ¼ cup

- Salt and ground black pepper to taste

- Tomato sauce – ½ cup, no sugar added

- Mayonnaise – ¼ cup

- Parmesan cheese -1/4 cup, grated

- Green bell pepper – 1 tbsp. seeded and chopped

- Pepperoni slices – 6, chopped

- Italian seasoning – ½ tsp.

- Black olives – 4, pitted and chopped

Method

1. In a bowl, mix cream cheese with mozzarella cheese, mayonnaise, sour cream, salt and pepper and mix well.

2. Spread into 4 ramekins, add a layer of tomato sauce, then layer parmesan cheese, and top with bell pepper, pepperoni, Italian seasoning, and black olives.

3. Place in an oven at 350F and bake for 20 minutes.

4. Serve.

Nutritional Facts Per Serving

- Calories: 284

- Fat: 24.4g

- Carb: 9.5g

- Protein: 8.6g

Flaxseed and Almond Muffins

Prep Time: 10 minutes

Cook Time: 15 minutes

Serving: 20

Ingredients

- Flaxseed meal – ½ cup

- Almond flour – ½ cup

- Swerve – 3 tbsp.

- Psyllium powder – 1 tbsp.

- A pinch of salt

- Olive oil cooking spray

- Baking powder – ¼ tsp.

- Egg – 1

- Coconut milk – ¼ cup

- Sour cream – 1/3 cup

- Hot dogs – 4, cut into 20 pieces

Method

1. In a bowl, mix flaxseed meal with flour, psyllium powder, swerve, salt, baking powder, and stir.

2. Add sour cream, egg, coconut milk, and whisk.

3. Grease a muffin tray with cooking oil, divide this batter.

4. Place a hot dog piece in the middle of each muffin.

5. Place in an oven at 350F, and bake for 12 minutes.

6. Broil in preheated broiler for 3 minutes, then divide onto a platter.

7. Serve.

Nutritional Facts Per Serving

• Calories: 65

• Fat: 3.4g

• Carb: 7.1g

• Protein: 1.7g

Fried Queso

Prep Time: 10 minutes

Cook Time: 10 minutes

Serving: 6

Ingredients

- Olives – 2 ounces, pitted and chopped

- Queso Blanco – 5 ounces, cubed and slightly frozen

- A pinch of red pepper flakes

- Olive oil – 1 ½ tbsp.

Method

1. Heat a pan with oil over medium heat.

2. Add queso cubes, and cook until bottom melts a bit.

3. Flip cubes with a spatula, and sprinkle black olives on top.

4. Let the cubes cook a bit more, flip again, sprinkle with red pepper flakes, and cook until crispy.

5. Flip, cook on the other side until crispy. Transfer to a cutting board, and cut into small blocks.

6. Serve.

Nutritional Facts Per Serving

- Calories: 152

- Fat: 15.8g

- Carb: 1g

- Protein: 3.2g

Maple and Pecan Bars

Prep Time: 10 minutes

Cook Time: 25 minutes

Serving: 12

Ingredients

- Flaxseed meal – ½ cup

- Pecans – 2 cups, toasted, and crushed

- Almond flour – 1 cup

- Coconut oil – ½ cup

- Stevia – ¼ tsp.

- Coconut – ½ cup, shredded

- Keto maple syrup – ¼ cup

For the keto maple syrup

- Erythritol – ¼ cup

- Coconut oil – 2 ¼ tsp.

- Butter – 1 tbsp.

- Xanthan gum – ¼ tsp.

- Water – ¾ cup

- Maple extract – 2 tsp.

- Vanilla extract – ½ tsp.

Method

1. In a bowl, mix butter with 2 ¼ tsp coconut oil and xanthan gum, stir, place in a microwave, and heat up for 1 minute.

2. Add erythritol, maple, water, vanilla extract, and stir well.

3. Heat in a microwave for 1 minute.

4. In a bowl, mix the flaxseed meal with coconut and almond flour. Stir.

5. Add pecans and stir again.

6. Add ¼-cup keto maple syrup, stevia, ½-cup coconut oil and stir well.

7. Spread in a baking dish, press well.

8. Place in an oven at 350F, and bake for 25 minutes.

9. Cool and cut into 12 bars.

10.Serve.

Nutritional Facts Per Serving

• Calories: 313

• Fat: 31.1g

• Carb: 8.8g

• Protein: 2.7g

Baked Chia Seeds

Prep Time: 10 minutes

Cook Time: 35 minutes

Serving: 36

Ingredients

- Ice water – 1 ¼ cup

- Chia seeds – ½ cup, ground

- Cheddar cheese – 3 ounces, grated

- Xanthan gum – ¼ tsp.

- Olive oil – 2 tbsp.

- Psyllium husk powder – 2 tbsp.

- Dried oregano – ¼ tsp.

- Garlic powder – ¼ tsp.

- Onion powder – ¼ tsp.

- Salt and ground black pepper to taste

- Sweet paprika – ¼ tsp.

Method

1. In a bowl, mix chia seeds with psyllium powder, xanthan gum, oregano, garlic, onion powder, paprika, salt, pepper, and stir.

2. Add oil and stir well. Add ice water and stir until you get a firm dough.

3. Spread this on a baking sheet.

4. Place in an oven at 350F and bake for 35 minutes.

5. Cool, cut and serve.

Nutritional Facts Per Serving

- Calories: 11

- Fat: 1g

- Carb: 0.1g

- Protein: 0.6g

Avocado Dip

Prep Time: 3 hours

Cook Time: 10 minutes

Serving: 4

Ingredients

- Erythritol powder – ¼ cup

- Avocados – 2, pitted, peeled and cut into slices

- Stevia – ¼ tsp.

- Fresh cilantro – ½ cup, chopped

- Juice and zest of 2 limes

- Coconut milk – 1 cup

Method

1. Place the avocado slices on a lined baking sheet, squeeze half of the lime juice over them, and keep in a freezer for 3 hours.

2. Heat the coconut milk in a pan over medium heat.

3. Add lime zest, stir, and bring to a boil.

4. Add erythritol powder, stir, take off heat, and set aside to cool.

5. Transfer avocado to a food processor, add the rest of the lime juice and the cilantro, and pulse well.

6. Add coconut milk mixture and stevia, and blend well.

7. Serve.

Nutritional Facts Per Serving

• Calories: 352

• Fat: 33.9g

• Carb: 7.3g

• Protein: 3.3g

Prosciutto Wrapped Shrimp

Prep Time: 10 minutes

Cook Time: 20 minutes

Serving: 16

Ingredients

- Olive oil – 2 tbsp.

- Cooked shrimp – 10 ounces, peeled and deveined

- Fresh mint – 1 tbsp. chopped

- Erythritol – 2 tbsp.

- Blackberries – 1/3 cup, mashed

- Prosciutto – 11 slices

- Red wine – 1/3 cup

Method

1. Wrap each shrimp in prosciutto slices.

2. Arrange on a lined baking sheet, drizzle olive oil over them.

3. Place in an oven at 425F and bake for 15 minutes.

4. Heat a pan with mashed blackberries over medium heat.

5. Add wine, mint, and erythritol.

6. Stir-fry for 3 minutes and remove from heat.

7. Arrange shrimp on a platter.

8. Drizzle blackberry sauce over them and serve.

Nutritional Facts Per Serving

- Calories: 89

- Fat: 5.5g

- Carb: 1.1g

- Protein: 10.1g

Chapter 9: Fish and Seafood Recipes

Shrimp and Cucumber Noodle Salad

Prep Time: 10 minutes

Cook Time: 0 minutes

Serving: 4

Ingredients

- Cucumber – 1, cut with a spiralizer

- Fresh basil – ½ cup, chopped

- Cooked shrimp – ½ pound, peeled and deveined

- Salt and ground black pepper to taste

- Stevia – 1 tbsp.

- Fish sauce – 2 tsp.

- Lime juice – 2 tbsp.

- Tomato paste – 2 tsp.

- Chili powder – ½ tsp.

Method

1. Put cucumber noodles on a paper towel, cover with another paper towel and press well.

2. Put into a bowl and mix with basil, shrimp, salt, and pepper.

3. In another bowl, mix stevia with fish sauce, lime juice, chili powder, and tomato paste and whisk.

4. Add to the shrimp salad, toss to coat well, and serve.

Nutritional Facts Per Serving

- Calories: 84

- Fat: 1.1g

- Carb: 5.2g

- Protein: 13.8g

Roasted Mahi Mahi and Tomato

Prep Time: 10 minutes

Cook Time: 16 minutes

Serving: 2

Ingredients

- Mahi-Mahi – 3 fillets

- Onion – ½ cup, chopped

- Olive oil – 4 tsp.

- Greek seasoning – 1 tsp.

- Garlic – 1 tsp. minced

- Green bell pepper – 1, chopped

- Tomato paste – ½ cup, no sugar added

- Kalamata olives – 2 tbsp. pitted and chopped

- Chicken stock – ¼ cup

- Salt and ground black pepper to taste

- Feta cheese – 2 tbsp. crumbled

Method

1. Heat a pan with 2 tsp oil over medium heat.

2. Add bell pepper and onion. Stir-fry for 3 minutes.

3. Add Greek seasoning and garlic. Stir-fry for 1 minute.

4. Add stock, olives, and tomato paste. Stir-fry for 5 minutes or until mixture thickens. Transfer to a bowl and set aside.

5. Heat the pan again with the rest of the oil.

6. Add the fish, season with salt and pepper. Cook for 2 minutes.

7. Flip, cook for 2 minutes, and transfer to a baking dish.

8. Spoon salsa over fish, place in an oven.

9. Bake for 425F for 6 minutes.

10. Sprinkle feta on top and serve.

Nutritional Facts Per Serving

- Calories: 368

- Fat: 14.4g

- Carb: 7.6g

- Protein: 42.2g

Spicy Shrimp

Prep Time: 10 minutes

Cook Time: 8 minutes

Serving: 2

Ingredients

• Shrimp – ½ pound, peeled and deveined

• Worcestershire sauce – 2 tsp.

• Olive oil – 2 tsp.

• Juice of 1 lemon

• Salt and black pepper to taste

• Creole seasoning – 1 tsp.

Method

1. Arrange shrimp in one layer in a baking dish.

2. Season with salt, pepper, and drizzle the oil.

3. Add Worcestershire sauce, lemon juice, and sprinkle with seasoning.

4. Toss shrimp in the seasoning, place in an oven, set it under the broiler.

5. Broil for 8 minutes.

6. Divide between 2 plates and serve.

Nutritional Facts Per Serving

- Calories: 192

- Fat: 6.7g

- Carb: 6.6g

- Protein: 26.3g

Shrimp Stew

Prep Time: 10 minutes

Cook Time: 15 minutes

Serving: 6

Ingredients

- Onion – ¼ cup, peeled and chopped

- Olive oil – ¼ cup

- Garlic – 1 clove, peeled and minced

- Shrimp – 1 ½ pounds, peeled and deveined

- Red pepper – ¼ cup, roasted and chopped

- Canned diced tomatoes – 14 ounces

- Fresh cilantro – ¼ cup, chopped

- Sriracha sauce – 2 tbsp.

- Coconut milk – 1 cup

- Salt and ground black pepper to taste

- Lime juice – 2 tbsp.

Method

1. Heat a pan with oil over medium heat.

2. Add onion and stir-fry for 4 minutes.

3. Add peppers and garlic. Stir-fry for 4 minutes.

4. Add tomatoes, cilantro, shrimp, and stir-fry until shrimp turns pink.

5. Add coconut milk and sriracha sauce, stir and bring to a gentle simmer.

6. Add the salt, pepper, lime juice, stir and transfer to bowls.

7. Serve.

Nutritional Facts Per Serving

- Calories: 376

- Fat: 25.1g

- Carb: 2.5g

- Protein: 46.3g

Garlicky Mussels

Prep Time: 5 minutes

Cook Time: 5 minutes

Serving: 4

Ingredients

• Mussels – 2 pounds, de-bearded and scrubbed

• Garlic – 2 cloves, peeled and minced

• Butter – 1 tbsp.

• A splash of lemon juice

Method

1. Put some water in a saucepan, add mussels.

2. Bring to a boil and cook for 5 minutes.

3. Remove from heat, discard any unopened mussels, and transfer them to a bowl.

4. In another bowl, mix butter with garlic and lemon juice, whisk, and heat in the microwave for 1 minute.

5. Pour over mussels and serve.

Nutritional Facts Per Serving

- Calories: 224

- Fat: 8g

- Carb: 9g

- Protein: 27.2g

Fried Calamari with Spicy Sauce

Prep Time: 10 minutes

Cook Time: 20 minutes

Serving: 2

Ingredients

- Squid – 1, cut into medium rings

- A pinch of cayenne pepper

- Egg – 1, whisked

- Coconut flour – 2 tbsp.

- Salt and ground black pepper to taste

- Coconut oil for frying

- Lemon juice – 1 tbsp.

- Mayonnaise – 4 tbsp.

- Sriracha sauce – 1 tsp.

Method

1. Season squid rings with salt, pepper and cayenne pepper, and put them in a bowl.

2. In another bowl, mix the egg with salt, pepper, coconut flour, and whisk. Coat the calamari rings in the egg mixture.

3. Heat a pan with enough coconut oil over medium heat.

4. Add calamari rings, and cook them until they become golden brown on both sides.

5. Transfer to paper towels, drain excess grease, and put in a bowl.

6. In another bowl, mix mayonnaise with lemon juice and sriracha sauce, and stir well.

7. Serve the calamari rings with this sauce on the side.

Nutritional Facts Per Serving

- Calories: 620

- Fat: 42.9g

- Carb: 5.7g

- Protein: 40g

Octopus Salad

Prep Time: 10 minutes

Cook Time: 40 minutes

Serving: 2

Ingredients

• Octopus – 21 ounces, rinsed

• Juice of 1 lemon

• Celery - 4 stalks, chopped

• Olive oil – 3 tbsp

• Salt and ground black pepper to taste

• Fresh parsley – 4 tbsp. chopped

Method

1. Put the octopus in a pot, add enough water to cover. Place a lid on the pot.

2. Bring to a boil over medium heat, and cook for 40 minutes. Drain and set aside to cool.

3. Chop octopus and put it in a salad bowl.

4. Add parsley, celery stalks, oil, lemon juice, and toss well.

5. Season with salt and pepper.

6. Toss again and serve.

Nutritional Facts Per Serving

- Calories: 839

- Fat: 46g

- Carb: 5.6g

- Protein: 89.3g

Clam Chowder

Prep Time: 10 minutes

Cook Time: 2 hours

Serving: 4

Ingredients

- Celery stalks – 1 cup, chopped

- Salt and black pepper to taste

- Ground thyme – 1 tsp.

- Chicken stock – 2 cups

- Canned baby clams – 14 ounces

- Heavy cream – 2 cups

- Onion – 1 cup, peeled and chopped

- Bacon slices – 12, chopped

Method

1. Heat a pan over medium heat.

2. Add bacon slices and brown all over. Transfer bacon to a bowl. Reserve the bacon grease in the pan.

3. Heat the pan again, add celery onion, stir, and cook for 5 minutes.

4. Transfer everything, including the bacon, to a slow cooker with the baby clams, salt, pepper, stock, thyme, and cream. Stir, and cook on high for 2 hours.

5. Divide into bowls and serve.

Nutritional Facts Per Serving

- Calories: 583

- Fat: 46.6g

- Carb: 7.2g

- Protein: 23.8g

Salmon Rolls

Prep Time: 10 minutes

Cook Time: 0 minutes

Serving: 12

Ingredients

• Nori sheets – 2

• Small avocado – 1, pitted, peeled, and diced

• Smoked salmon – 6 ounces, sliced

• Cream cheese – 4 ounces

• Cucumber – 1, sliced

• Wasabi paste - 1 tsp.

• Pickled ginger for serving

Method

1. Place a nori sheet on a sushi mat.

2. Divide salmon slices, avocado, and cucumber slices between them. In a bowl, mix cream cheese with wasabi paste and stir well.

3. Spread over cucumber slices, roll the nori sheets. Press well.

4. Cut each into 6 pieces, and serve with pickled ginger.

Nutritional Facts Per Serving

- Calories: 89

- Fat: 7.2g

- Carb: 2.6g

- Protein: 4g

Salmon Skewers

Prep Time: 10 minutes

Cook Time: 8 minutes

Serving: 4

Ingredients

- Salmon fillet – 12 ounces, cubed

- Onion – 1, chopped into chunked

- Red bell pepper – ½, chopped

- Green bell pepper – ½, chopped

- Orange bell pepper – ½, chopped

- Juice from 1 lemon

- Salt and ground black pepper to taste

- A drizzle of olive oil

Method

1. Thread skewers with onion, bell peppers, and salmon cubes.

2. Season with salt and pepper. Drizzle them with oil and lemon juice, and place them on a preheated grill over medium heat.

3. Cook for 4 minutes on each side, divide onto plates.

4. Serve.

Nutritional Facts Per Serving

- Calories: 162

- Fat: 5.6g

- Carb: 11.6g

- Protein: 18g

Cod Salad

Prep Time: 2 hours

Cook Time: 20 minutes

Serving: 8

Ingredients

- Jarred pimiento peppers – 2 cups, chopped

- Salted cod – 2 pounds

- Fresh parsley – 1 cup, chopped

- Kalamata olives – 1 cup, pitted, and chopped

- Capers – 6 tbsp.

- Olive oil – ¾ cup

- Salt and ground black pepper to taste

- Juice from 2 lemons

- Garlic cloves – 4, peeled and minced

- Celery stalks – 2, chopped

- Red chili flakes – ½ tsp.

- Escarole head – 1, leaves separated

Method

1. Put cod in a saucepan, add water to cover.

2. Bring to a boil over medium heat, boil for 20 minutes, drain and cut into medium chunks.

3. Put cod in a salad bowl, add parsley, peppers, olives, capers, celery, garlic, lemon juice, salt, pepper, olive oil, chili flakes, and toss to coat.

4. Arrange the escarole leaves on a platter, and add the cod salad.

5. Serve.

Nutritional Facts Per Serving

- Calories: 342

- Fat: 22.1g

- Carb: 3.6g

- Protein: 33.1g

Sardine Salad

Prep Time: 5 minutes

Cook Time: 0 minutes

Serving: 1

Ingredients

• Canned sardines in oil – 5 ounces

• Lemon juice – 1 tbsp.

• Small cucumber – 1, chopped

• Mustard – ½ tbsp.

• Salt and ground black pepper to taste

Method

1. Drain sardines. Put them in a bowl and mash with a fork.

2. Add salt, pepper, cucumber, lemon juice, and mustard.

3. Mix and serve.

Nutritional Facts Per Serving

- Calories: 509

- Fat: 32.5g

- Carb: 8.3g

- Protein: 42.1g

Italian Clam Delight

Prep Time: 10 minutes

Cook Time: 10 minutes

Serving: 6

Ingredients

- Butter – ½ cup

- Clams – 36, scrubbed

- Red pepper flakes – 1 tsp.

- Fresh parsley – 1 tsp. chopped

- Garlic – 5 cloves, peeled and minced

- Dried oregano – 1 tbsp.

- White wine – 2 cups

Method

1. Heat a pan with butter.

2. Add garlic and stir-fry for 1 minute.

3. Add oregano, parsley, wine, pepper flakes, and stir well.

4. Add clams, stir, cover and cook for 10 minutes.

5. Discard any unopened clams, ladle clam mixture into bowls.

6. Serve.

Nutritional Facts Per Serving

- Calories: 287

- Fat: 15.8g

- Carb: 2.2g

- Protein: 5g

Lemon-Glazed Salmon

Prep Time: 10 minutes

Cook Time: 10 minutes

Serving: 2

Ingredients

- Lemons – 2, sliced

- Wild salmon – 1 pound, skinless and cubed

- Balsamic vinegar – ¼ cup

- Lemon juice – ¼ cup

- Coconut oil – 1 tsp.

- No sugar added lemon marmalade – 1/3 cup

Method

1. Heat a pot over medium heat.

2. Add lemon juice, vinegar, marmalade, stir well and bring to a simmer for 1 minute.

3. Lower heat and cook until mixture thickens a bit. Remove from heat.

4. Arrange salmon and lemon slices on skewers, and brush them on one side with the lemon glaze.

5. Brush a kitchen grill with coconut oil and heat over medium heat.

6. Place salmon kebabs on grill glazed side down and cook for 4 minutes.

7. Flip the kebabs, brush with the rest of the orange glaze, cook for 4 minutes and serve.

Nutritional Facts Per Serving

- Calories: 332

- Fat: 13.3g

- Carb: 2.5g

- Protein: 34.1g

Tuna and Chimichurri Sauce

Prep Time: 10 minutes

Cook Time: 5 minutes

Serving: 4

Ingredients

- Fresh cilantro – ½ cup, chopped

- Olive oil – 1/3 cup plus 2 tbsp.

- Onion – 1, chopped

- Balsamic vinegar – 3 tbsp.

- Fresh parsley – 2 tbsp. chopped

- Fresh basil – 2 tbsp. chopped

- Jalapeno pepper - 1, chopped

- Sushi-grade tuna steak – 1 pound

- Salt and ground black pepper to taste

- Red pepper flakes – 1 tsp.

- Fresh thyme – 1 tsp. chopped

- A pinch of cayenne pepper

- Garlic – 3 cloves, minced

- Avocados – 2, sliced

- Baby arugula – 6 ounces

Method

1. In a bowl, mix 1/3 cup oil with jalapeno, onion, vinegar, basil, cilantro, garlic, parsley, pepper flakes, cayenne, thyme, salt, pepper, and whisk and set aside.

2. Heat a pan with remaining oil over medium-high heat.

3. Add tuna, season with salt, and pepper.

4. Cook for 2 minutes on each side.

5. Cool and slice.

6. Mix arugula with half of the chimichurri mixture and toss to coat.

7. Divide arugula onto plates, top with tuna slices.

8. Drizzle the rest of the chimichurri sauce.

9. Serve with avocado slices on the side.

Nutritional Facts Per Serving

- Calories: 564

- Fat: 37.6g

- Carb: 3.8g

- Protein: 48.6g

Chapter 10: Poultry Recipes

Creamy Chicken

Prep Time: 10 minutes

Cook Time: 1 hour

Serving: 4

Ingredients

- Chicken breasts – 4, skinless and boneless

- Mayonnaise – ½ cup

- Sour cream – ½ cup

- Salt and ground black pepper to taste

- Parmesan cheese – ¾ cup, grated

- Mozzarella cheese – 8 slices

Method

1. Spray a baking dish, place chicken breasts in and top each piece with 2 mozzarella cheese slices.

2. In a bowl, mix Parmesan cheese with salt, pepper, mayonnaise, garlic powder, sour cream, and set aside.

3. Spread over the chicken, place the dish in the oven at 375F and bake for 1 hour.

4. Serve.

Nutritional Facts Per Serving

- Calories: 525

- Fat: 49.7g

- Carb:8.6 g

- Protein: 55g

Chicken and Broccoli Casserole

Prep Time: 10 minutes

Cook Time: 50 minutes

Serving: 4

Ingredients

• Cheddar cheese – 3 cups, grated

• Broccoli florets – 10 ounces

• Chicken breasts – 3, skinless, boneless, cooked and cubed

• Mayonnaise -1 cup

• Coconut oil – 1 tbsp. melted

• Chicken stock - 1/3 cup

• Salt and ground black pepper to taste

• Juice of 1 lemon

Method

1. Grease a baking dish with oil, and arrange chicken pieces on the bottom.

2. Spread broccoli florets, then half the cheese.

3. In a bowl, mix mayo with stock, salt, pepper, and lemon juice.

4. Pour over the chicken, sprinkle rest of the cheese. Cover the dish with aluminum foil, and bake in the oven at 350F for 30 minutes.

5. Remove aluminum foil, and bake for 20 minutes.

6. Serve.

Nutritional Facts Per Serving

- Calories: 414

- Fat: 67g

- Carb: 9.9g

- Protein: 87g

Creamy Chicken Soup

Prep Time: 10 minutes

Cook Time: 20 minutes

Serving: 4

Ingredients

- Butter – 3 tbsp.

- Cream cheese – 4 ounces

- Chicken – 2 cups, cooked and shredded

- Chicken stock – 4 cups

- Salt and black pepper to taste

- Sour cream – ½ cup

- Celery – ¼ cup, chopped

Method

1. In a blender, mix stock with cream cheese, butter, salt, pepper, sour cream, and pulse well.

2. Transfer to a saucepan, heat over medium heat, add celery and chicken.

3. Stir, simmer for a few minutes.

4. Divide into bowls and serve.

Nutritional Facts Per Serving

• Calories: 381

• Fat: 30g

• Carb: 2.9g

• Protein: 24g

Four-Cheese Chicken

Prep Time: 10 minutes

Cook Time: 50 minutes

Serving: 4

Ingredients

- Chicken breasts – 3 pounds

- Muenster cheese – 2 ounces, cubed

- Cream cheese – 2 ounces

- Cheddar cheese – 4 ounces, cubed

- Provolone cheese - 2 ounces, cubed

- Zucchini – 1, shredded

- Salt and ground black pepper to taste

- Garlic – 1 tsp. minced

- Bacon – ½ cup, cooked and crumbled

Method

1. Season zucchini with salt and pepper. Set aside for a few minutes, squeeze well and transfer to a bowl.

2. Add bacon, garlic, more salt, pepper, cream cheese, cheddar cheese, Muenster cheese, and provolone cheese. Stir.

3. Cut slits into chicken breasts, season with salt, pepper, and stuff with zucchini and cheese mixture.

4. Place on a lined baking sheet.

5. Place in an oven at 400F and bake for 45 minutes.

6. Serve.

Nutritional Facts Per Serving

• Calories: 479

• Fat: 67g

• Carb: 3.8g

• Protein: 57g

Crusted Chicken

Prep Time: 10 minutes

Cook Time: 35 minutes

Serving: 4

Ingredients

- Bacon – 4 slices, cooked and crumbled

- Chicken breasts – 4, skinless and boneless

- Water – 1 tbsp.

- Avocado oil – ½ cup

- Egg – 1, whisked

- Salt and ground black pepper to taste

- Asiago cheese – 1 cup, shredded

- Garlic powder – ¼ tsp.

- Parmesan cheese – 1 cup, grated

Method

1. In a bowl, mix Parmesan cheese with garlic, salt, pepper, and stir.

2. Put the whisked egg in another bowl and mix with the water.

3. Season chicken with salt and pepper, dip each piece into egg, and then into cheese mixture.

4. Heat a pan with oil.

5. Add chicken breasts and cook until golden on both sides. Transfer to a baking pan.

6. Place in an oven at 350F, and bake for 20 minutes.

7. Top chicken with bacon and cheese, place in the oven, turn on the broiler, and broil for 2 minutes.

8. Serve hot.

Nutritional Facts Per Serving

- Calories: 355

- Fat: 44g

- Carb: 3.1g

- Protein: 47g

Orange Chicken

Prep Time: 10 minutes

Cook Time: 15 minutes

Serving: 4

Ingredients

• Chicken thighs – 2 pounds, skinless, boneless, and cut into pieces

• Salt and ground black pepper to taste

• Coconut oil – 3 tbsp.

• Coconut flour – ¼ cup

For the sauce

• Fish sauce – 2 tbsp.

• Lemon zest – 1 ½ tsp.

• Fresh ginger - 1 tbsp. grated

• Orange juice – ¼ cup, no sugar added

• Stevia – 2 tsp.

- Sesame seeds – ¼ tsp.

- Scallions – 2 tbsp. chopped

- Coriander – ½ tsp.

- Water – 1 cup

- Red pepper flakes – ¼ tsp.

- Liquid aminos – 2 tbsp.

Method

1. In a bowl, mix coconut flour, salt, pepper, and stir.

2. Add chicken pieces and toss to coat well.

3. Heat a pan with oil. Add chicken, and cook until golden brown on both sides. Transfer to a bowl.

4. In a blender, mix orange juice with ginger, fish sauce, liquid aminos, stevia, lemon zest, water, and coriander and blend well.

5. Pour into a pan and heat over medium heat.

6. Add chicken, stir, and cook for 2 minutes.

7. Add sesame seeds, scallions, and pepper flakes. Stir-fry for 2 minutes. Remove from heat.

8. Serve.

Nutritional Facts Per Serving

- Calories: 542

- Fat: 27.4g

- Carb: 4.3g

- Protein: 65g

Bacon-Wrapped Chicken

Prep Time: 10 minutes

Cook Time: 35 minutes

Serving: 4

Ingredients

- Fresh chives – 1 tbsp. chopped

- Cream cheese – 8 ounces

- Chicken breasts – 2 pounds, skinless, and boneless

- Bacon slices – 12

- Salt and ground black pepper to taste

Method

- Heat a pan over medium heat.

- Add bacon and cook until halfway done. Transfer to paper towels and drain the grease.

- In a bowl, mix cream cheese with salt, pepper, chives, and stir.

- Use a meat tenderizer to flatten the chicken breasts, add cream cheese mixture, roll them, and wrap each in a bacon slice.

- Arrange wrapped chicken breasts in a baking dish.

- Place in an oven at 375F and bake for 30 minutes.

- Serve.

Nutritional Facts Per Serving

- Calories: 937

- Fat: 60g

- Carb: 2.4g

- Protein: 91g

Turkey Sushi

Prep Time: 5 minutes

Cook Time: 0 minutes

Serving: 4

Ingredients

• Roast deli turkey – 12 slices (about 4 ounces)

• Mayonnaise – ½ cup, plus 2 tbsp.

• Provolone cheese – 12 slices

• Tomato – 12 thin slices

• Arugula – 1 cup, micro salad greens, or torn lettuce leaves of choice

Method

1. Place a slice of turkey on a clean work surface with the short end facing you.

2. Spread 2 ½ tsp of mayo on the turkey.

3. Top with a slice of provolone cheese and then a slice of tomato.

4. Arrange the greens across the top of the tomato.

5. Roll it up like a sushi roll and slice into 1-inch pieces.

6. Serve.

Nutritional Facts Per Serving

- Calories: 406

- Fat: 31.1g

- Carb: 5.4g

- Protein: 24.6g

Bacon Wrapped Turkey Meatballs

Prep Time: 10 minutes

Cook Time: 35 minutes

Serving: 10

Ingredients

• Bacon – 10 slices

• Pork rinds – 1 oz, powdered

• Spinach – 1 cup, chopped and divided

• Thyme – 3 sprigs

• Small red chilies – 3

• Small onion – 1, chopped

• Green pepper – ½, chopped

• Ground turkey – 2 lb.

• Salt – 1 tsp.

• Ground black pepper – ½ tsp.

• Eggs – 2

Method

1. Preheat the oven to 380F. Lay your bacon slices on a baking sheet lined with a foil. Cook for 20 minutes.

2. Grind the pork rinds into powder with a food processor. Then grind ½ cup of spinach, thyme, red chilies, onion, and green pepper.

3. Pour the resulting mixture in a bowl.

4. Add ground turkey, salt, black pepper, and mix.

5. Add the eggs and mix well.

6. Now remove and set aside the bacon and drain off any surplus grease from the baking sheet.

7. From the turkey, make 10 meatballs and put them on the baking sheet.

8. Bake for 15 minutes or until juices run clear.

9. Meanwhile, make the spinach 'butter' by adding remaining ½ cup spinach to the rendered bacon fat.

10. Process the mixture until everything is combined.

11. Wrap each meatball with the slice of bacon and tie using the toothpick.

12.Serve with a small spoon of the spinach 'butter'.

Nutritional Facts Per Serving

• Calories: 316

• Fat: 26.3g

• Carb: 2.1g

• Protein: 21.4g

Turkey, Avocado, and Umami Wraps

Prep Time: 10 minutes

Cook Time: 45 minutes

Serving: 4

Ingredients

- Turkey breast steaks – 4

- Umami paste – 4 tsp.

- Parmesan cheese – 1 cup, grated

- Small avocado – 1, sliced

- Ghee or butter – 4 tbsp.

- Pinch of pink Himalayan salt

- Olive oil for spraying

Method

1. Preheat the oven to 400F.

2. Flatten the turkey steaks with a meat tenderizer.

3. Spread 1 tsp. of umami paste over each slice of meat.

4. Add grated parmesan cheese and slices of avocado.

5. Wrap up tightly.

6. Grease a baking dish with ghee and place the wraps on it (seam side down).

7. Spray some olive oil over it.

8. Cover with a lid or parchment paper and transfer into the oven.

9. Bake for 40 to 45 minutes.

10. Remove the lid 10 minutes before it is done.

11. Serve.

Nutritional Facts Per Serving

- Calories: 428

- Fat: 27.1g

- Carb: 3.2g

- Protein: 43.1g

Crispy Duck Legs with Braised Vegetables

Prep Time: 10 minutes

Cook Time: 1 hours and 20 minutes

Serving: 2

Ingredients

- Duck legs - 2

- Salt and pepper to taste

- Chopped zucchini - 1 cup

- Cubed rutabaga – 1 cup

- Brussels sprouts – 1 cup, trimmed and quartered

- Onion – ½, diced

- Chicken stock – 2 cups

Method

1. Preheat the oven to 400F.

2. In a skillet, put the duck legs (skin-side down) and set over medium heat.

3. Sprinkle with salt and pepper and cook for 10 minutes or until brown and crisp.

4. Flip legs and cook for another 1 to 2 minutes. Then remove to a plate.

5. Add vegetables to the pan. Season with salt and pepper and cook until beginning to brown, about 10 to 15 minutes.

6. Add the duck legs into the vegetables, skin side up.

7. Add stock so the legs are submerged halfway.

8. Increase heat to medium and bring to a simmer.

9. Bake in the skillet for 30 minutes.

10. Lower the heat to 350F and bake for another 30 minutes.

11. Remove and serve.

Nutritional Facts Per Serving

- Calories: 558

- Fat: 49g

- Carb: 9g

- Protein: 17g

Roasted Duck in Wine Sauce

Prep Time: 10 minutes

Cook Time: 60 minutes

Serving: 6

Ingredients

- One frozen duck – 4.5 lb. defrosted

- Olive oil – 2 tbsp.

- Garlic powder – 1 tsp.

- Italian seasoning – 1 tsp. (thyme, oregano, basil)

- Ground turmeric – 1 tsp.

- White button mushrooms – 5 to 6, sliced thick

- White onion – 1 large, sliced

- White wine – 1 cup

Method

1. Rub olive oil all over the duck.

2. Sprinkle the duck with the turmeric. Then sprinkle garlic powder and Italian seasonings over.

3. Place the duck in a roasting bag and add 1 cup of white wine.

4. Add the onion and mushrooms into the middle of the duck.

5. Seal the roasting bag and place into a roasting pan.

6. Place in a 350F oven and cook for 60 minutes.

7. To make the wine sauce: mix one or two tbsp coconut flour with the gravy in a bowl. Mix and serve.

Nutritional Facts Per Serving

- Calories: 154.3

- Fat: 8g

- Carb: 2.2g

- Protein: 8.7g

Chinese Duck with Orange Sauce

Prep Time: 5 minutes

Cook Time: 25 minutes

Serving: 2

Ingredients

- Duck breasts – 2

- Salt – 1 tsp.

- Pepper – ½ tsp.

- Chinese 5 spice – 1.5 tsp.

Sauce

- Chicken stock – 1 cup

- Xylitol – 2 tbsp.

- Tamari – 4 tbsp.

- Chinese 5 spice – ½ tsp.

- Cinnamon – ½ tsp.

- Apple cider vinegar – 2 tsp.

- Peel of one orange

Method

1. Preheat the oven to 400F.

2. Combine all the sauce ingredients in a small saucepan.

3. Simmer the sauce for 20 to 25 minutes on low heat while you prepare the duck. Whisk occasionally.

4. To prepare the duck, combine salt, pepper, and 5 spice.

5. Score the duck skin (similar to crisscross pattern).

6. Rub the duck breast well with the spice mixture.

7. Heat a pan and place the duck breasts skin side down.

8. Cook for 5 minutes, then turn and cook for 2 minutes more. Drain off the fat.

9. Cook the duck in the oven for 8 to 10 minutes.

10. Remove from the oven. Cover with a foil and rest. Discard the orange peel.

11. Serve with a salad.

Nutritional Facts Per Serving

- Calories: 358

- Fat: 11g

- Carb: 9g

- Protein: 52g

Chicken with Olive Tapenade

Prep Time: 10 minutes

Cook Time: 10 minutes

Serving: 2

Ingredients

- Chicken breast – 1, cut into 4 pieces

- Coconut oil – 2 tbsp.

- Garlic – 3 cloves, peeled, and crushed

- Olive tapenade – ½ cup

For the tapenade

- Black olives – 1 cup, pitted

- Salt and black pepper to taste

- Olive oil – 2 tbsp.

- Fresh parsley – ¼ cup, chopped

- Lemon juice – 1 tbsp.

Method

1. In a food processor, mix olives with salt, pepper, 2 tbsp. olive oil, lemon juice, and parsley. Blend well and transfer to a bowl.

2. In a pan, heat the coconut oil and add garlic. Stir-fry for 2 minutes.

3. Add chicken pieces and cook for 4 minutes on each side.

4. Divide chicken on plates and top with the olive tapenade.

Nutritional Facts Per Serving

- Calories: 727

- Fat: 61g

- Carb: 7.5g

- Protein: 37.7g

Baked Turkey Delight

Prep Time: 10 minutes

Cook Time: 45 minutes

Serving: 8

Ingredients

- Zucchini – 4 cups, cut with a spiralizer

- Egg – 1, whisked

- Cabbage – 3 cups, shredded

- Turkey meat – 3 cups, cooked and shredded

- Turkey stock - ½ cup

- Cream cheese – ½ cup

- Poultry seasoning – 1 tsp.

- Cheddar cheese – 2 cups, grated

- Parmesan cheese – ½ cup, grated

- Salt and ground black pepper to taste

- Garlic powder – ¼ tsp.

Method

1. Heat a pan with stock over medium-low heat.

2. Add cream, egg, Parmesan cheese, cheddar cheese, salt, pepper, poultry seasoning, and garlic powder. Mix and bring to a simmer.

3. Add turkey meat, cabbage, stir and take off the heat.

4. Place zucchini noodles in a baking dish, add some salt and pepper, add the turkey mixture and spread.

5. Cover with aluminum foil, place in an oven at 400F, and bake for 35 minutes.

6. Cool and serve.

Nutritional Facts Per Serving

- Calories: 290

- Fat: 18.5g

- Carb: 4.6g

- Protein: 26.4g

Chapter 11: Meat Recipes

Roasted Pork Belly

Prep Time: 10 minutes

Cook Time: 1 hours and 30 minutes

Serving: 6

Ingredients

• Stevia – 2 tbsp.

• Lemon juice – 1 tbsp.

• Water – 4 cups

• Chayote squash – 17 ounces, cored, and cut into wedges

• Pork belly – 2 pounds, scored

• Salt and black pepper to taste

• A drizzle of olive oil

Method

1. In a blender, mix water with squash, lemon juice, and stevia, pulse well.

2. Put pork belly in a steamer tray and steam for 1 hour.

3. Transfer pork belly to a baking sheet, rub with a drizzle of oil, season with salt and pepper and pour squash sauce over it.

4. Place in an oven at 425F for 30 minutes.

5. Slice pork roast, divide onto plates and serve.

Nutritional Facts Per Serving

- Calories: 723

- Fat: 40.7g

- Carb: 5.9g

- Protein: 70.6g

Stuffed Pork

Prep Time: 10 minutes

Cook Time: 30 minutes

Serving: 4

Ingredients

• Zest of 2 limes

• Zest of 1 lemon

• Juice from 1 lemon

• Juice from 2 limes

• Garlic – 4 tsp, minced

• Olive oil – ¾ cup

• Fresh cilantro – 1 cup, chopped

• Fresh mint – 1 cup, chopped

• Dried oregano – 1 tsp.

• Salt and ground black pepper to taste

• Cumin – 2 tsp.

- Pork loin steaks – 4

- Pickles – 2, chopped

- Ham slices – 4

- Swiss cheese slices – 6

- Mustard – 2 tbsp.

Method

1. In a food processor, mix lime juice, lime zest, lemon zest, lemon juice, oil, garlic, cilantro, mint, cumin, oregano, salt, pepper, and blend well.

2. Season steaks with salt and pepper. Place them into a bowl, add marinade, toss to coat, and set aside for 2 hours.

3. Place steaks on a work surface.

4. Divide pickles, cheese, mustard, and ham onto them, roll and secure with toothpicks.

5. Heat a pan over medium-high heat, add pork rolls, and cook for 2 minutes on each side. Transfer to a baking sheet.

6. Place in the oven at 350F, and bake for 25 minutes.

7. Serve.

Nutritional Facts Per Serving

- Calories: 1157

- Fat: 75g

- Carb: 4.6g

- Protein: 113.2g

Lemon and Garlic Pork

Prep Time: 10 minutes

Cook Time: 30 minutes

Serving: 4

Ingredients

- Butter – 3 tbsp.

- Pork steaks – 4, bone-in

- Chicken stock – 1 cup

- Salt and ground black pepper to taste

- A pinch of lemon pepper

- Coconut oil – 3 tbsp.

- Garlic – 6 cloves, peeled and minced

- Fresh parsley – 2 tbsp. chopped

- Mushrooms – 8, chopped

- Lemon – 1, sliced

Method

1. Heat a pan with 2 tbsp. oil and 2 tbsp. butter over medium heat.

2. Add pork steaks, season with salt, and pepper and cook until brown on both sides. Transfer to a plate.

3. Return pan to medium heat, and rest of the butter, oil, and half of the stock. Stir well, and cook for 1 minute.

4. Add garlic, and mushrooms, and stir-fry for 4 minutes.

5. Add lemon slices, rest of the stock, salt, pepper, and lemon pepper. Stir-fry for 5 minutes.

6. Return pork steaks to pan and cook everything for 10 minutes.

7. Divide steaks and sauce on plates and serve.

Nutritional Facts Per Serving

- Calories: 665

- Fat: 49.2g

- Carb: 5g

- Protein: 47.6g

Jamaican Pork

Prep Time: 10 minutes

Cook Time: 45 minutes

Serving: 12

Ingredients

- Pork shoulder – 4 pounds

- Coconut oil – 1 tbsp.

- Beef stock – ½ cup

- Jamaican jerk spice mix – ¼ cup

Method

- Rub pork shoulder with Jamaican mixture.

- Add oil to an Instant Pot, and set it to sauté more.

- Add pork shoulder and brown on all sides.

- Add stock, cover Instant Pot and cook on Meat/Stew mode for 45 minutes.

- Open and shred the meat.

- Serve.

Nutritional Facts Per Serving

- Calories: 452

- Fat: 33.5g

- Carb: 0g

- Protein: 35.3g

Juicy Pork Chops

Prep Time: 10 minutes

Cook Time: 45 minutes

Serving: 4

Ingredients

- Onions – 2, peeled and chopped

- Bacon slices – 6, chopped

- Chicken stock – ½ cup

- Salt and ground black pepper to taste

- Pork chops - 4

Method

1. Heat a pan over medium heat.

2. Add bacon and stir-fry until crispy. Transfer to a bowl.

3. Return pan to medium heat.

4. Add onions, and some salt and pepper. Stir, cover, and cook for 15 minutes. Transfer to the same bowl with bacon.

5. Return to heat, increase to medium-high.

6. Add pork chops, season with salt and pepper.

7. Brown for 3 minutes on one side. Flip, reduce heat to medium and cook for 7 minutes.

8. Return bacon and onions to the pan, stir, and cook for 1 minute.

9. Divide on plates and serve.

Nutritional Facts Per Serving

• Calories: 433

• Fat: 31.9g

• Carb: 5.6g

• Protein: 29.2g

Beef Patties

Prep Time: 10 minutes

Cook Time: 35 minutes

Serving: 6

Ingredients

• Cauliflower rice – ½ cup

• Egg – 1

• Salt and ground black pepper to taste

• Ground beef – 1 ½ pounds

• Canned onion soup – 10 ounces

• Coconut flour – 1 tbsp.

• Ketchup – ¼ cup, no sugar added

• Worcestershire sauce – 3 tsp.

• Dry mustard – ½ tsp.

• Water – ¼ cup

Method

1. In a bowl, mix 1/3 cup of onion soup with beef, salt, pepper, egg, cauliflower rice, and stir well.

2. Heat a pan over medium heat.

3. Shape 6 patties from beef mixture, place into the pan, and brown on both sides.

4. In a bowl, mix rest of the soup with coconut flour, water, dry mustard, Worcestershire sauce, ketchup, and stir well.

5. Pour over the beef patties, cover pan, and cook for 20 minutes. Stir occasionally.

6. Divide on plates and serve.

Nutritional Facts Per Serving

• Calories: 846

• Fat: 28.2g

• Carb: 10.1g

• Protein: 130.3g

Beef Meatballs Casserole

Prep Time: 10 minutes

Cook Time: 50 minutes

Serving: 8

Ingredients

- Almond flour – 1/3 cup

- Eggs – 2

- Beef sausage – 1 pound, chopped

- Ground beef – 1 pound

- Salt and ground black pepper to taste

- Dried parsley – 1 tbsp.

- Red pepper flakes – ¼ tsp.

- Parmesan cheese – ¼ cup, grated

- Onion powder – ¼ tsp.

- Garlic powder – ½ tsp.

- Dried oregano – ¼ tsp.

- Ricotta cheese – 1 cup

- Tomato paste – 2 cups, no sugar added

- Minced garlic – 2 tsp.

- Dried basil – 2 tsp.

- Dried rosemary – 1 tsp.

- Mozzarella cheese – 1 ½ cup, shredded

Method

1. In a bowl, mix sausage with beef, almond flour, salt, pepper, parsley, pepper flakes, onion powder, garlic powder, oregano, parmesan cheese, eggs, and stir well.

2. Shape meatballs, and place on a lined baking sheet.

3. Place in an oven at 375F, and bake for 15 minutes.

4. Take meatballs out of the oven, transfer to a baking dish, and cover with half of the tomato paste, garlic, basil, and rosemary.

5. Add ricotta cheese all over and then pour over the rest of the tomato mixture.

6. Sprinkle mozzarella cheese all over, place the dish in the oven at 375F and bake for 30 minutes.

7. Remove, cool and serve.

Nutritional Facts Per Serving

- Calories: 531

- Fat: 33.6g

- Carb: 7.5g

- Protein: 40.6g

Beef and Tomato-Stuffed Squash

Prep Time: 10 minutes

Cook Time: 1 hour

Serving: 2

Ingredients

- Spaghetti squash – 1 pound, pricked with a fork

- Salt and ground black pepper to taste

- Garlic – 3 cloves, peeled and minced

- Onion – 1, chopped

- Portobello mushroom – 1, sliced

- Canned diced tomatoes – 28 ounces

- Dried oregano – 1 tsp.

- Cayenne pepper – ¼ tsp.

- Dried thyme – ½ tsp.

- Ground beef – 1 pound

- Green bell pepper – 1, seeded and chopped

Method

1. Place squash on a lined baking sheet.

2. Place in the oven at 400F and bake for 40 minutes.

3. Cut in half, set aside to cool. Remove seeds and leave aside.

4. Heat a pan over medium-high heat.

5. Add meat, onion, garlic, mushroom, stir-fry until meat browns.

6. Add thyme, salt, pepper, oregano, cayenne, tomatoes, green pepper, stir and cook for 10 minutes.

7. Stuff squash halves with beef mixture.

8. Place in an oven at 400F and bake for 10 minutes.

9. Serve.

Nutritional Facts Per Serving

- Calories: 616

- Fat: 16.6g

- Carb: 7.1g

- Protein: 75.5g

Beef Goulash

Prep Time: 10 minutes

Cook Time: 20 minutes

Serving: 5

Ingredients

- Bell pepper – 2 ounces, seeded and chopped

- Ground beef – 1 ½ pounds

- Salt and ground black pepper to taste

- Cauliflower florets – 2 cups

- Onion – ¼ cup, peeled and chopped

- Canned diced tomatoes – 14 ounces

- Garlic powder – ¼ tsp.

- Tomato paste – 1 tbsp.

- Water – 14 ounces

Method

1. Heat a pan over medium heat.

2. Add beef, stir and brown for 5 minutes.

3. Add bell pepper and onion. Stir-fry for 4 minutes.

4. Add tomatoes, cauliflower, water, stir, bring to a simmer, cover, and cook for 5 minutes.

5. Add garlic powder, tomato paste, salt, pepper, stir, and remove from the heat.

6. Serve.

Nutritional Facts Per Serving

- Calories: 972

- Fat: 31.4g

- Carb: 10.1g

- Protein: 153g

Braised Lamb Chops

Prep Time: 10 minutes

Cook Time: 2 hours and 20 minutes

Serving: 4

Ingredients

- Lamb chops - 8

- Garlic powder – 1 tsp.

- Salt and ground black pepper to taste

- Fresh mint – 2 tsp. crushed

- A drizzle of olive oil

- Shallot – 1, peeled and chopped

- White wine – 1 cup

- Juice of ½ lemon

- Bay leaf – 1

- Beef stock – 2 cups

- Fresh parsley, chopped, for serving

For the sauce

- Cranberries – 2 cups

- Fresh rosemary – ½ tsp, chopped

- Swerve – ½ cup

- Dried mint – 1 tsp.

- Juice of ½ lemon

- Fresh ginger – 1 tsp, grated

- Water – 1 cup

- Harissa paste – 1 tsp.

Method

1. In a bowl, mix lamb chops with 1 tsp garlic powder, 2 tsp mint, salt, pepper and rub well.

2. Heat a pan with oil and add lamb chops. Brown on all sides, and transfer to a plate.

3. Heat the same pan again over medium heat.

4. Add shallots, stir and cook for 1 minute.

5. Add wine and bay leaf, stir, and cook for 4 minutes.

6. Add 2 cups beef stock, parsley, and juice from ½ lemon. Stir and simmer for 5 minutes.

7. Return lamb, stir, and cook for 10 minutes.

8. Cover the pan, and place it in the oven at 350F for 2 hours.

9. Heat a pan over medium-high heat.

10. Add cranberries, swerve, rosemary, the juice from ½ lemon, 1 tsp. mint, ginger, water, harissa paste, stir, and bring to a simmer for 15 minutes.

11. Take lamb chops out of the oven, divide them on plates.

12. Drizzle cranberry sauce over them.

13. Serve.

Nutritional Facts Per Serving

- Calories: 1148

- Fat: 42g

- Carb: 7.6g

- Protein: 160g

Lamb Salad

Prep Time: 10 minutes

Cook Time: 35 minutes

Serving: 4

Ingredients

• Olive oil – 1 tbsp.

• Leg of lamb – 3 pounds, bone removed, and leg butterflied

• Salt and ground black pepper to taste

• Cumin - 1 tsp.

• A pinch of dried thyme

• Garlic – 2 cloves, peeled and minced

For the salad

• Feta cheese – 4 ounces, crumbled

• Pecans – ½ cup

• Spinach – 2 cups

- Lemon juice – 1 ½ tbsp.

- Olive oil – ¼ cup

- Fresh mint – 1 cup, chopped

Method

1. Rub lamb with salt, pepper, 1 tbsp oil, thyme, cumin, and minced garlic.

2. Place on the preheated grill pan over medium heat and cook for 40 minutes. Flip once.

3. Spread pecans on a lined baking sheet.

4. Place in an oven at 350F and toast for 10 minutes.

5. Transfer grilled lamb to a cutting board, set aside to cool down, and slice.

6. In a salad bowl, mix spinach with 1-cup mint, feta cheese, ¼-cup olive oil, lemon juice, toasted pecans, salt, and pepper.

7. Toss to coat.

8. Add lamb slices on top and serve.

Nutritional Facts Per Serving

- Calories: 931

- Fat: 52.5g

- Carb: 8.3g

- Protein: 103.7g

Moroccan Lamb

Prep Time: 10 minutes

Cook Time: 15 minutes

Serving: 4

Ingredients

- Paprika – 2 tsp.

- Garlic – 2 cloves, minced

- Dried oregano – 2 tsp.

- Sumac – 2 tbsp.

- Lamb cutlets - 12

- Olive oil – ¼ cup

- Water – 2 tbsp.

- Cumin – 2 tsp.

- Butternut squash – 10 oz, peeled and sliced

- Fresh parsley - ¼ cup, chopped

- Harissa – 2 tsp.

- Red wine vinegar – 1 tbsp.

- Salt and ground black pepper to taste

- Black olives – 2 tbsp. pitted and sliced

- Radishes – 6, sliced thinly

Method

1. In a bowl, mix cutlets with garlic, paprika, oregano, sumac, salt, pepper, half of the oil and water. Rub well.

2. Put squash in a pot, add water to cover, bring to a boil over medium heat.

3. Cook for 2 minutes and drain. Put in a bowl.

4. Add olives and radishes to squash.

5. In another bowl, mix harissa with remaining oil, parsley, cumin, vinegar, a splash of water and stir well.

6. Add to squash mixture, season with salt and pepper and toss to coat.

7. Heat a kitchen grill over medium-high heat.

8. Add lamb cutlets; grill them for 3 minutes on each side.

9. Divide them on plates, add squash salad and serve.

Nutritional Facts Per Serving

- Calories: 737

- Fat: 37.7g

- Carb: 2.2g

- Protein: 92.4g

Lamb Curry

Prep Time: 10 minutes

Cook Time: 4 hours

Serving: 6

Ingredients

- Fresh ginger – 2 tbsp, grated

- Garlic – 2 cloves, peeled and minced

- Cardamom – 2 tsp.

- Onion – 1, peeled and hopped

- Cloves – 6

- Lamb meat – 1 pound, cubed

- Cumin powder – 2 tsp.

- Garam masala – 1 tsp.

- Chili powder – ½ tsp.

- Turmeric – 1 tsp.

- Coriander – 2 tsp.

- Spinach – 1 pound

- Canned diced tomatoes – 14 ounces

Method

1. In a slow cooker, mix lamb with tomatoes, spinach, ginger, garlic, onion, cardamom, cloves, cumin, garam masala, chili, turmeric, and coriander.

2. Stir, cover and cook on high for 4 hours.

3. Uncover slow cooker, stir the chili, divide into bowls, and serve.

Nutritional Facts Per Serving

- Calories: 186

- Fat: 6.1g

- Carb: 9.1g

- Protein: 24.3g

Lamb Stew

Prep Time: 10 minutes

Cook Time: 3 hours

Serving: 4

Ingredients

- Onion – 1, peeled and chopped

- Butternut squash – 7 oz. peeled and chopped

- Lamb – 2 pounds, cubed

- Tomato – 1, cored and chopped

- Garlic – 1 clove, peeled and minced

- Butter – 2 tbsp.

- Beef stock – 1 cup

- White wine – 1 cup

- Salt and ground black pepper to taste

- Rosemary sprigs – 2

- Fresh thyme – 1, chopped

Method

1. Heat a Dutch Oven over medium heat. Add oil and heat up.

2. Add lamb, salt, and pepper, brown on all sides and transfer to a plate.

3. Add onion to the Dutch Oven and cook for 2 minutes.

4. Add tomato, squash, garlic, butter, stock, wine, salt, pepper, rosemary, thyme. Stir and cook for 2 minutes.

5. Return lamb to Dutch Oven, stir, and reduce heat to medium-low.

6. Cover and cook for 4 hours.

7. Discard rosemary sprigs. Taste and adjust seasoning.

8. Serve.

Nutritional Facts Per Serving

- Calories: 564

- Fat: 22.6g

- Carb: 11g

- Protein: 65.5g

Sausage Stew

Prep Time: 10 minutes

Cook Time: 20 minutes

Serving: 9

Ingredients

- Smoked sausage – 1 pound, sliced

- Green bell pepper – 1, chopped

- Onions – 2, chopped

- Salt and ground black pepper to taste

- Fresh parsley – 1 cup, chopped

- Green onions – 8, chopped

- Avocado oil – ¼ cup

- Beef stock – 1 cup

- Garlic – 6 cloves

- Canned diced tomatoes – 28 ounces

- Okra – 16 ounces, trimmed and sliced

- Tomato paste – 8 ounces, no sugar added

- Coconut aminos – 2 tbsp.

- Cayenne pepper powder – 1 tbsp.

Method

- Heat a pot with oil over medium-high heat.

- Add sausages, and stir-fry for 2 minutes.

- Add bell pepper, onion, green onions, parsley, salt, and pepper. Stir-fry for 2 minutes.

- Add garlic, stock, okra, tomatoes, coconut aminos, tomato paste, cayenne pepper, stir and bring to a simmer. Cook for 15 minutes.

- Taste and adjust seasoning.

- Serve.

Nutritional Facts Per Serving

- Calories: 253

- Fat: 15.7g

- Carb: 5.2g

- Protein: 13.2g

Chapter 12: Vegetable Recipes

Arugula and Broccoli Soup

Prep Time: 10 minutes

Cook Time: 20 minutes

Serving: 4

Ingredients

- Onion – 1, chopped

- Olive oil - 1 tbsp.

- Garlic – 1 clove, minced

- Broccoli – 1 head, separated into florets

- Salt and black pepper to taste

- Vegetable stock – 2 ½ cups

- Cumin – 1 tsp.

- Juice of ½ lemon

- Arugula leaves – 1 cup

Method

1. Heat oil in a saucepan over medium heat.

2. Add onions, and stir-fry for 4 minutes.

3. Add garlic and cook for 1 minute.

4. Add cumin, broccoli, salt, and pepper. Stir-fry for 4 minutes.

5. Add stock, stir, and cook for 8 minutes.

6. Blend soup with a hand mixer. Add half of the arugula, and blend again.

7. Add the rest of the arugula, stir, and heat up soup again.

8. Add lemon juice, stir, and ladle into soup bowls.

9. Serve.

Nutritional Facts Per Serving

- Calories: 74
- Fat: 4.9g
- Carb: 8.8g
- Protein: 2.5g

Zucchini Cream

Prep Time: 10 minutes

Cook Time: 25 minutes

Serving: 8

Ingredients

- Zucchini – 6, cut in half and sliced

- Salt and black pepper to taste

- Butter – 1 tbsp.

- Vegetable stock – 28 ounces

- Dried oregano – 1 tsp.

- Onion – ½ cup, chopped

- Garlic – 3 cloves, minced

- Parmesan cheese – 2 ounces, grated

- Heavy cream – ¾ cup

Method

1. Heat a saucepan with butter over medium heat.

2. Add onion, stir, and cook for 4 minutes.

3. Add garlic, stir, and cook for 2 minutes.

4. Add zucchini, stir, and cook for 3 minutes.

5. Add stock, stir, bring to a boil, and simmer over medium heat for 15 minutes.

6. Add salt, oregano, pepper, stir, take off heat, and blend with a hand mixer.

7. Heat soup again, add heavy cream, stir, and bring to a simmer.

8. Add Parmesan cheese, stir, take off heat, ladle into bowls.

9. Serve.

Nutritional Facts Per Serving

- Calories: 109

- Fat: 7.5g

- Carb: 7.5g

- Protein: 4.9g

Zucchini and Avocado Soup

Prep Time: 10 minutes

Cook Time: 15 minutes

Serving: 4

Ingredients

- Big avocado – 1, chopped

- Scallions – 4, chopped

- Fresh ginger – 1 tsp. chopped

- Avocado oil – 2 tbsp.

- Salt and ground black pepper to taste

- Zucchinis – 2, chopped

- Vegetable stock – 29 ounces

- Garlic – 1 clove, minced

- Water – 1 cup

- Lemon juice – 1 tbsp.

- Red bell pepper – 1, chopped

Method

1. Heat oil in a saucepan over medium heat.

2. Add onions, stir, and cook for 3 minutes.

3. Add ginger, and garlic, and stir-fry for 1 minute.

4. Add zucchini, salt, pepper, water, stock, and stir.

5. Bring to a boil, cover pan, and cook for 10 minutes.

6. Remove from heat, set soup aside for 2 minutes.

7. Add avocado, stir, blend with a hand mixer and heat up again.

8. Add more salt and pepper if needed.

9. Add lemon juice and bell pepper. Stir, and heat up soup again.

10. Serve.

Nutritional Facts Per Serving

- Calories: 155

- Fat: 11.1g

- Carb: 6.4g

- Protein: 3.7g

Swiss Chard Salad

Prep Time: 10 minutes

Cook Time: 20 minutes

Serving: 4

Ingredients

- Swiss chard – 1 bunch, cut into strips

- Avocado oil – 2 tbsp.

- Onion – 1, peeled and chopped

- A pinch of red pepper flakes

- Pine nuts – ¼ cup, toasted

- Balsamic vinegar – 1 tbsp.

- Salt and ground black pepper to taste

Method

1. Heat a pan with oil over medium heat.

2. Add chard and onions. Stir-fry for 5 minutes.

3. Add pepper flakes, salt, and pepper. Stir-fry for 3 minutes.

4. Add pine nuts to the pan with vinegar. Stir-fry for 3 minutes.

5. Serve.

Nutritional Facts Per Serving

• Calories: 80

• Fat: 6.8g

• Carb: 4.6g

• Protein: 1.8g

Catalan-Style Greens

Prep Time: 10 minutes

Cook Time: 15 minutes

Serving: 4

Ingredients

- Onion – 1, sliced

- Avocado oil – 3 tbsp.

- Prunes – ¼ cup

- Garlic – 6 cloves, chopped

- Pine nuts – ¼ cup, toasted

- Balsamic vinegar – ¼ cup

- Swiss chard – 2 ½ cups

- Spinach – 2 ½ cups

- Salt and ground black pepper to taste

- A pinch of nutmeg

Method

1. Heat a pan with oil over medium heat.

2. Add onion. Stir-fry for 7 minutes.

3. Add garlic and stir-fry for 1 minute.

4. Add vinegar, chopped prunes, spinach, chard, stir and cook for 5 minutes.

5. Add salt, pepper, nutmeg and cook for a few seconds.

6. Serve.

Nutritional Facts Per Serving

- Calories: 154

- Fat: 7.8g

- Carb: 9.1g

- Protein: 6.1g

Fried Parmesan Tomatoes

Prep Time: 7 minutes

Cook Time: 6 minutes

Serving: 4

Ingredients

- Coconut oil – 4 tbsp.

- Eggs – 2

- Grated Parmesan cheese – ½ cup

- Yellow or green tomato – 1 large, sliced

Method

1. Heat the coconut oil in a saucepan.

2. Beat the eggs in a bowl.

3. Place the grated parmesan in another bowl.

4. Dip each slice of tomato into the egg to coat, then into Parmesan.

5. Place the cheese-coated tomato slices in the hot oil.

6. Fry until the cheese is golden brown on each side of the tomato.

Nutritional Facts Per Serving

- Calories: 209

- Fat: 19g

- Carb: 2.3g

- Protein: 7g

Creamy "mac"-n-Cheese

Prep Time: 5 minutes

Cook Time: 25 minutes

Serving: 6

Ingredients

- Unsalted butter – ¼ cup

- Very thinly sliced cabbage – 4 cups

For the cheese sauce

- Unsalted butter – ¼ cup

- Cream cheese – 1 ½ ounces

- Vegetable broth – ¼ cup

- Shredded sharp cheddar cheese – 1 cup

- Grated parmesan cheese – ¼ cup

- Fine sea salt and fresh ground black pepper

- Diced tomato – ½ cup

Method

1. Place the sliced cabbage and butter into a sauté pan over medium heat and cook until very tender, about 15 minutes. Stirring often.

2. Remove from the heat and set aside.

3. Make the cheese sauce: in a saucepan, melt the butter over medium heat.

4. Stir in the cream cheese and broth.

5. Cook, stirring constantly, for 2 minutes.

6. Reduce heat to low and add the Parmesan cheese and cheddar.

7. Cook and stir until the cheese melts. Add salt and pepper to taste.

8. Remove the cheese sauce from the heat.

9. Pour over the cabbage pasta and stir to combine.

10.Garnish with yellow tomatoes and serve.

Nutritional Facts Per Serving

- Calories: 241

- Fat: 23.3g

- Carb: 1.8g

- Protein: 7.5g

Brown Butter Mushrooms

Prep Time: 5 minutes

Cook Time: 15 minutes

Serving: 4

Ingredients

• Button or cremini mushrooms - 1 pound, cleaned

• Unsalted butter – ¼ cup

• Chopped fresh herbs – 2 tsp.

• Fine sea salt – ½ tsp.

Method

1. Cook the mushrooms in a saucepan over medium heat until the mushrooms give up much of their liquid; about 10 minutes.

2. Meanwhile, heat up the butter in a saucepan over medium heat until it sizzles and brown flecks appear.

3. Continue to cook and whisk for 5 minutes, until the butter is dark golden brown. Remove from heat and add herbs.

4. Pour off the liquid from the mushroom pan and reserve broth.

5. Pour the browned butter onto the mushrooms and cook for 5 minutes or until they are golden brown.

6. Season with salt and serve immediately.

Nutritional Facts Per Serving

- Calories: 131

- Fat: 11.4g

- Carb: 4.8g

- Protein: 3g

Creamy coleslaw

Prep Time: 8 minutes

Cook Time: 1 hour

Serving: 6

Ingredients

- Shredded cabbage – 4 cups

- Thinly sliced yellow onion – ¼ cup

For the dressing

- Mayonnaise – ½ cup

- Powdered erythritol – 1/3 cup

- Stevia glycerite – ¼ tsp.

- Dill pickle juice – ¼ cup

- Lemon juice – 2 ½ tbsp.

- Celery seeds – ½ tsp.

- Fine sea salt – ½ tsp.

- Fresh ground black pepper – 1/8 tsp.

Method

1. In a bowl, combine the cabbage and onion. Set aside.

2. In another bowl, combine the ingredients for the dressing and mix well.

3. Pour the dressing over the cabbage and onion and gently stir to coat in the dressing.

4. Refrigerate for 1 hour before serving.

Nutritional Facts Per Serving

- Calories: 162

- Fat: 13.6g

- Carb: 9.4g

- Protein: 2.1g

Onion Rings

Prep Time: 10 minutes

Cook Time: 30 minutes

Serving: 6

Ingredients

• Sweet onions – 3 large

• Bacon – 24 slices, thin-cut

• Ranch dressing – 1 cup

Method

1. Preheat the oven to 375F. Line a rimmed baking sheet with parchment paper.

2. Slice the onions into 2/3 inch thick rings.

3. Wrap each onion ring tightly in bacon and use a toothpick to hold it in place.

4. Place the wrapped onion rings on the rimmed baking sheet and bake for 25 to 30 minutes or until bacon is crispy.

5. Serve with a dipping sauce.

Nutritional Facts Per Serving

- Calories: 242

- Fat: 16.1g

- Carb: 7.9g

- Protein: 15.5g

Avocado Fries II

Prep Time: 10 minutes

Cook Time: 15 minutes

Serving: 6

Ingredients

• Firm, barely ripe avocados – 3

• Thin-cut bacon – 1 pound

• Taco seasoning – 1 tbsp.

• Salsa – ½ cup, for serving

Method

1. Preheat the oven to 425F.

2. Line a rimmed baking sheet with parchment paper.

3. Peel and pit the avocados. Then slice them into thick-cut French fry shapes.

4. Wrap each slice with bacon and secure with a toothpick.

5. Season with taco seasoning.

6. Bake for 12 to 14 minutes or until bacon is crisp.

7. Serve with salsa.

Nutritional Facts Per Serving

- Calories: 635

- Fat: 51.6g

- Carb: 12g

- Protein: 30.6g

Chapter 13: Dessert Recipes

Peanut Butter and Chocolate Brownies

Prep Time: 10 minutes

Cook Time: 30 minutes

Serving: 4

Ingredients

- Egg - 1

- Cocoa powder – 1/3 cup

- Erythritol – 1/3 cup

- Butter – 7 tbsp.

- A pinch of salt

- Vanilla extract – ½ tsp.

- Almond flour – ¼ cup

- Walnuts – ¼ cup

- Baking powder – ½ tsp.

- Peanut butter – 1 tbsp.

Method

1. Heat a pan with 6 tbsp. butter and erythritol over medium heat.

2. Stir and cook for 5 minutes.

3. Transfer to a bowl. Add salt, vanilla extract, cocoa powder, and whisk.

4. Add egg and stir well.

5. Add baking powder, almond flour, walnuts, and stir well. Pour into a skillet.

6. In a bowl, mix 1 tbsp. butter with peanut butter. Heat in a microwave for a few seconds and stir well.

7. Drizzle over brownie mixture in the skillet.

8. Place in an oven at 350F and bake for 30 minutes.

9. Cool, slice and serve.

Nutritional Facts Per Serving

- Calories: 300

- Fat: 30.2g

- Carb: 9.1g

- Protein: 6.4g

Blueberry Scones

Prep Time: 10 minutes

Cook Time: 10 minutes

Serving: 10

Ingredients

- Coconut flour – ½ cup

- Blueberries – 1 cup

- Eggs – 2

- Heavy cream – ½ cup

- Butter – ½ cup

- Almond flour – ½ cup

- A pinch of salt

- Stevia – 5 tbsp.

- Vanilla extract – 2 tsp.

- Baking powder – 2 tsp.

Method

1. In a bowl, mix coconut flour and almond flour, salt, baking powder, blueberries, and stir well.

2. In another bowl, mix butter, heavy cream, vanilla extract, stevia, eggs, and stir well.

3. Combine the 2 mixtures, and stir until you get a dough.

4. Shape 10 triangles from the mixture and place on a lined baking sheet.

5. Place in an oven at 350F and bake for 10 minutes.

6. Serve.

Nutritional Facts Per Serving

- Calories: 199

- Fat: 16g

- Carb: 10.6g

- Protein: 4g

Chocolate Cookies

Prep Time: 10 minutes

Cook Time: 40 minutes

Serving: 12

Ingredients

- Vanilla extract – 1 tsp.

- Butter – ½ cup

- Egg – 1

- Monk fruit sweetener – 2 tbsp.

- Swerve – ¼ cup

- A pinch of salt

- Almond flour – 2 cups

- Unsweetened chocolate chips – ½ cup

Method

1. Heat a pan with butter over medium heat. Stir, and cook until it browns. Remove from heat and set aside for 5 minutes.

2. In a bowl, mix the egg with vanilla extract, monk fruit extract, swerve, and stir.

3. Add melted butter, flour, salt, half the chocolate chips, and stir.

4. Transfer to a pan. Spread the rest of the chocolate chips on top.

5. Place in an oven at 350F and bake for 30 minutes.

6. Cool, slice and serve.

Nutritional Facts Per Serving

• Calories: 172

• Fat: 15.8g

• Carb: 3.8g

• Protein: 3.4g

Peach Cake

Prep Time: 10 minutes

Cook Time: 20 minutes

Serving: 12

Ingredients

- Eggs - 6

- Peaches – 2, stoned, cut into quarters

- Vanilla extract – 1 tsp.

- Baking powder – 1 tsp.

- Almond meal – 9 ounces

- Swerve – 4 tbsp.

- A pinch of salt

- Orange zest – 2 tbsp.

- Stevia – 2 ounces

- Cream cheese – 4 ounces

- Plain Greek yogurt – 4 ounces

Method

1. Pulse peaches in a food processor.

2. Add swerve, almond meal, eggs, baking powder, vanilla extract, a pinch of salt, and pulse well. Transfer into 2 spring-form pans.

3. Place in an oven at 350F and bake for 20 minutes.

4. In a bowl, mix cream cheese with yogurt, orange zest, stevia, and stir well.

5. Place one cake layer on a plate, add half of the cream cheese mixture, add the other cake layer, and top with the rest of the cream cheese mixture.

6. Spread it well. Slice and serve.

Nutritional Facts Per Serving

- Calories: 207

- Fat: 16.5g

- Carb: 8.6g

- Protein: 8.7g

Lemon Custard

Prep Time: 10 minutes

Cook Time: 30 minutes

Serving: 6

Ingredients

• Almond milk – 2 ½ cups

• Lemon zest - 4 tbsp.

• Eggs – 4

• Swerve – 5 tbsp.

• Lemon juice – 2 tbsp.

Method

1. In a bowl, mix eggs with milk and swerve and stir well.

2. Add lemon zest and lemon juice. Whisk, pour into 6 ramekins and place into a baking dish with some water on the bottom.

3. Bake in the oven at 360F for 30 minutes.

4. Cool and serve.

Nutritional Facts Per Serving

- Calories: 111

- Fat: 5.7g

- Carb: 4g

- Protein: 4.9g

Caramel Custard

Prep Time: 10 minutes

Cook Time: 30 minutes

Serving: 2

Ingredients

- Caramel extract – 1 ½ tsp.

- Water – 1 cup

- Cream cheese – 2 ounces

- Eggs – 2

- Swerve – 1 ½ tbsp.

For the caramel sauce

- Swerve – 2 tbsp.

- Butter – 2 tbsp.

- Caramel extract – ¼ tsp.

Method

1. In a blender, mix cream cheese with water, 1 ½ tbsp. swerve, 1 ½ tsp. caramel extract, eggs, and blend well.

2. Pour into 2 greased ramekins and place in an oven at 350F and bake for 30 minutes.

3. Put butter into a saucepan and heat over medium heat.

4. Add ¼ tsp. caramel extract and 2 tbsp. swerve. Stir well and cook until everything melts.

5. Pour over caramel custard.

6. Cool and serve.

Nutritional Facts Per Serving

- Calories: 372

- Fat: 31g

- Carb: 11.3g

- Protein: 8.9g

Coconut Granola

Prep Time: 10 minutes

Cook Time: 35 minutes

Serving: 4

Ingredients

- Unsweetened coconut – 1 cup, shredded

- Almond and pecans – 1 cup, chopped

- Stevia – 2 tbsp.

- Pumpkin seeds – ½ cup

- Sunflower seeds – ½ cup

- Coconut oil – 2 tbsp.

- Ground nutmeg – 1 tsp.

- Cinnamon – ½ tsp.

- Ground nutmeg – 1/8 tsp.

- Ground allspice – 1/8 tsp.

Method

1. In a bowl, mix pecans, almonds, pumpkin seeds, sunflower seeds, coconut, nutmeg, ½ tsp. cinnamon, 1/8 tsp. ground nutmeg, 1/8 tsp. ground allspice, and stir well.

2. Heat a pan with coconut oil over medium heat.

3. Add stevia and stir well until combined.

4. Pour over nuts and coconut mixture and stir well.

5. Spread on a lined baking sheet.

6. Place in an oven at 300F and bake for 30 minutes.

7. Cool, cut and serve.

Nutritional Facts Per Serving

- Calories: 394

- Fat: 36g

- Carb: 8.4g

- Protein: 11.1g

Peanut Butter and Chia Pudding

Prep Time: 10 minutes

Cook Time: 0 minutes

Serving: 4

Ingredients

• Chia seeds – ½ cup

• Almond milk – 2 cups, unsweetened

• Vanilla extract – 1 ½ tsp.

• Peanut butter – ¼ cup, unsweetened

• Stevia – 1 tsp.

• A pinch of salt

Method

1. In a bowl, mix milk with chia seeds, peanut butter, vanilla extract, stevia, a pinch of salt, and mix well.

2. Leave pudding aside for 5 minutes, then stir it again.

3. Divide into dessert glasses, and leave in the refrigerator for 10 minutes.

4. Serve.

Nutritional Facts Per Serving

- Calories: 456

- Fat: 41.1g

- Carb: 6.5g

- Protein: 9.1g

No-Bake Cookies

Prep Time: 40 minutes

Cook Time: 2 minutes

Serving: 4

Ingredients

• Swerve – 1/5 cup

• Coconut milk – ¼ cup

• Coconut oil – ¼ cup

• Cocoa powder – 2 tbsp.

• Coconut – 1 ¾ cup, shredded

• Vanilla extract – ½ tsp.

• A pinch of salt

• Almond butter – ¾ cup

Method

1. Heat a pan with oil over medium heat.

2. Add milk, cocoa powder, swerve, stir well for 2 minutes and remove from heat.

3. Add a pinch of salt, vanilla extract, coconut, almond butter and stir well.

4. Place a spoonful of mixture on a lined baking sheet.

5. Cool in the refrigerator for 30 minutes and serve.

Nutritional Facts Per Serving

- Calories: 325

- Fat: 32.8g

- Carb: 5.8g

- Protein: 2.9g

Tiramisu Pudding

Prep Time: 2 hours

Cook Time: 0 minutes

Serving: 10

Ingredients

• Cream cheese – 8 ounces

• Cottage cheese – 16 ounces

• Unsweetened cocoa powder – 2 tbsp.

• Instant coffee – 1 tsp.

• Almond milk – 4 tbsp.

• Erythritol – ½ cup

Method

1. In a food processor, mix cottage cheese with cocoa powder, cream cheese, coffee, and blend well.

2. Add almond milk and erythritol, and blend again. Divide into dessert cups.

3. Keep in the refrigerator until you are ready to serve.

Nutritional Facts Per Serving

- Calories: 136

- Fat: 10.3g

- Carb: 8.2g

- Protein: 8.2g

Cherry and Chia Jam

Prep Time: 15 minutes

Cook Time: 12 minutes

Serving: 22

Ingredients

- Chia seeds – 3 tbsp.

- Cherries – 2 and ½ cups, pitted

- Vanilla extract – ½ tsp.

- Peel from – ½ lemon

- Erythritol – ¼ cup

- Stevia – 10 drops

- Water – 1 cup

Method

1. Put cherries and water in a saucepan.

2. Add other ingredients. Stir and bring to a simmer. Cook for 12 minutes.

3. Set jam aside for 15 minutes.

4. Serve.

Nutritional Facts Per Serving

- Calories: 26

- Fat: 1g

- Carb: 4.9g

- Protein: 1g

Almond Truffles

Prep Time: 1 hour and 15 minutes

Cook Time: 5 minutes

Serving: 24

Ingredients

• 75% or higher chocolate – 8 oz. chopped into small pieces

• Heavy cream – ½ cup

• Almond extract – 1 tsp.

• Unsweetened cocoa powder – ¼ cup

Method

1. Heat a saucepan over low heat.

2. Add heavy cream and bring to a simmer. Add almond extract and stir. Remove from the heat.

3. Pour hot cream over the chocolate pieces.

4. Wait for 1 minute and vigorously whisk until chocolate is fully melted and smooth.

5. Spread chocolate in a thin layer on a parchment-lined baking sheet.

6. Refrigerate for 1 hour.

7. Scoop 1-inch mounds of chocolate. Use your hands to quickly roll each mound into a smooth ball.

8. Immediately roll each ball in unsweetened cocoa powder. Place each in a small paper or foil wrapper.

9. Serve.

Nutritional Facts Per Serving

- Calories: 136

- Fat: 12g

- Carb: 5g

- Protein: 2g

Raspberry and Coconut Dessert

Prep Time: 10 minutes

Cook Time: 5 minutes

Serving: 12

Ingredients

- Coconut butter – ½ cup

- Coconut oil – ½ cup

- Raspberries – ½ cup, dried

- Swerve – ¼ cup

- Coconut – ½ cup, shredded

Method

1. Blend dried berries in a food processor.

2. Heat a pan with butter over medium heat.

3. Add oil, swerve, and coconut. Stir, and cook for 5 minutes.

4. Pour half into a lined baking pan and spread well.

5. Add raspberry mixture and spread well.

6. Top with remaining butter mixture, spread, and keep in the refrigerator for 2 hours.

7. Cut into pieces and serve.

Nutritional Facts Per Serving

- Calories: 124

- Fat: 13.1g

- Carb: 2.3g

- Protein: 1g

Vanilla Parfaits

Prep Time: 10 minutes

Cook Time: 0 minutes

Serving: 4

Ingredients

- Canned coconut milk – 14 ounces

- Vanilla extract – 1 tsp.

- Stevia – 10 drops

- Berries – 4 ounces

- Walnuts – 2 tbsp. chopped

Method

1. In a bowl, mix stevia with coconut milk and vanilla extract and whisk using a mixer.

2. In another bowl, mix berries with walnuts and stir.

3. Spoon half of vanilla coconut mixture into 4 jars, add a layer of berries, and top with rest of the vanilla mixture.

4. Top with berries and walnuts mixture.

5. Place in the refrigerator to chill before serving.

Nutritional Facts Per Serving

- Calories: 272

- Fat: 26g

- Carb: 9.5g

- Protein: 3.4g

Creamy Coconut Pudding

Prep Time: 4 hours and 10 minutes

Cook Time: 3 minutes

Serving: 2

Ingredients

• Gelatin – 4 tsp.

• Liquid stevia – ¼ tsp.

• Coconut milk – 1 cup

• A pinch of ground cardamom

• Ground ginger – ¼ tsp.

• Ground nutmeg – 1 pinch

Method

1. In a bowl, mix ¼ cup milk with gelatin, and stir well.

2. Put the rest of the coconut milk in a saucepan and heat.

3. Add gelatin mixture, stir and remove from heat. Set aside to cool, then keep in the refrigerator for 4 hours.

4. Transfer to a food processor, add stevia, cardamom, nutmeg, ginger, and blend for 2 minutes.

5. Divide into dessert cups and serve.

Nutritional Facts Per Serving

- Calories: 323

- Fat: 28.6g

- Carb: 6.7g

- Protein: 14.7g

Chapter 14: Condiments, Sauces, Dressings

Barbecue Sauce

Prep Time: 10 minutes

Cook Time: 30 minutes

Serving: 10

Ingredients

- Butter – 1 tbsp.

- Finely chopped onion – ½ cup

- Minced garlic – 1 ½ tbsp.

- Sugar-free cola – 1 ¼ cups

- Tomato paste – ¾ cup, no sugar added

- Water – ½ cup

- Sugar-free ketchup – ¼ cup

- Worcestershire sauce – 1 tbsp.

- Mustard – 3 tbsp.

- Cayenne pepper – 1 tsp.

- Liquid smoke – 1 tsp.

- Paprika – ½ tsp.

- Freshly ground black pepper – ½ tsp.

Method

1. Heat butter for 1 minute in a saucepan.

2. Add onion and cook for 4 minutes.

3. Add garlic and cook for 1 minute.

4. Add water, tomato paste, cola, ketchup, Worcestershire sauce, cayenne, mustard, liquid smoke, pepper, and paprika. Whisk to combine.

5. Bring the sauce to a simmer and cook for 25 minutes. Stir occasionally.

Nutritional Facts Per Serving (1 tbsp.)

- Calories: 47

- Fat: 2.2g

- Carb: 5.2g

- Protein: 1.7g

Teriyaki Sauce

Prep Time: 10 minutes

Cook Time: 15 minutes

Serving: 8

Ingredients

- Olive oil – 1/3 cup

- Minced garlic – 1 tsp.

- Minced fresh ginger – 1 tbsp.

- Liquid aminos – 1 cup

- Worcestershire sauce – 2 tbsp.

- White vinegar – 2 tbsp.

- Liquid stevia – 20 drops

- Ground black pepper – ½ tsp.

- Orange extract – ¼ tsp.

Method

1. In a large saucepan, heat the olive oil for 1 minute.

2. Add ginger and garlic and cook for 1 minute.

3. Add the Worcestershire sauce, liquid aminos, vinegar, stevia, pepper, and orange extract. Whisk to combine. Bring to a boil.

4. Lower heat and simmer and cook for 15 minutes or until reduced by half.

Nutritional Facts Per Serving (1 tbsp.)

- Calories: 110

- Fat: 8.4g

- Carb: 3.5g

- Protein: 4.1g

Sugar-Free Ketchup

Prep Time: 5 minutes

Cook Time: 0 minutes

Serving: 16

Ingredients

- Tomato paste – 1 ½ cups

- Water – ¼ cup

- Apple cider vinegar – 4 tbsp.

- Worcestershire sauce – 2 tbsp.

- Mustard – 1 tbsp.

- Salt – ½ tsp.

- Cinnamon – ½ tsp.

- Garlic powder – ¼ tsp.

- Freshly ground black pepper – 1/8 tsp.

- Ground cloves – 1/8 tsp.

Method

1. In a bowl, add everything and whisk to combine.

2. Chill and serve.

Nutritional Facts Per Serving (1 tbsp.)

- Calories: 24

- Fat: 0.3g

- Carb: 3.8g

- Protein: 1.1g

Blue Cheese Sauce

Prep Time: 10 minutes

Cook Time: 1 hour

Serving: 8

Ingredients

- Butter – 1 tbsp.

- Almond flour – 1 tbsp.

- Chicken broth – ½ cup

- Heavy (whipping) cream – ½ cup

- Unsweetened almond milk – ¼ cup

- Bleu cheese – 4 ounces

Method

1. Melt the butter in a saucepan.

2. Add the almond flour and lower heat.

3. Cook for 2 to 3 minutes and whisk constantly.

4. Add the heavy cream, chicken broth, and almond milk. Whisk to combine.

5. Increase heat to medium.

6. Add the blue cheese. Whisk until cheese melts and sauce is creamy.

7. Pour the sauce into a bowl and place in the refrigerator to chill for a few hours.

8. Serve.

Nutritional Facts Per Serving (1 tbsp.)

- Calories: 98

- Fat: 8.9g

- Carb: 0.6g

- Protein: 3.5g

Ranch Dressing

Prep Time: 10 minutes

Cook Time: 1 hour

Serving: 16

Ingredients

- Mayonnaise – 1 cup

- Sour cream – 1 cup

- Buttermilk – ¼ cup

- Onion powder – 1 tbsp.

- Dried parsley – 1 tbsp.

- Garlic powder – 2 tsp.

- Salt – ½ tsp.

- Dried dill – ½ tsp.

- Mustard powder – ½ tsp.

- Celery salt – ¼ tsp.

Method

1. Add everything in a bowl. Whisk to mix well.

2. Refrigerate for 1 hour before serving.

Nutritional Facts Per Serving (1 tbsp.)

- Calories: 93

- Fat: 8g

- Carb: 4.8g

- Protein: 0.9g

Mustard Cream Sauce

Prep Time: 5 minutes

Cook Time: 10 minutes

Serving: 6

Ingredients

- Butter – 1 tbsp.

- Minced onion – 1 tbsp.

- Minced garlic – 1 tsp.

- Heavy (whipping) cream – ½ cup

- Sour cream – ½ cup

- Mustard – 1 tbsp.

- Salt – ¼ tsp.

- Freshly ground black pepper – 1/8 tsp.

Method

1. Melt the butter in a saucepan over low heat.

2. Add garlic and onion and cook for 5 minutes.

3. Add the sour cream and heavy cream. Whisk until the consistency begins to thin.

4. Whisk in the mustard, salt, and pepper. Remove from heat.

5. Cool and refrigerate.

Nutritional Facts Per Serving (1 tbsp.)

• Calories: 103

• Fat: 10.2g

• Carb: 1.9g

• Protein: 1.4g

Homemade Mayonnaise

Prep Time: 10 minutes

Cook Time: 0 minutes

Serving: 32

Ingredients

- Mustard powder – 2 tsp.

- Lemon juice – 2 tbsp. divided

- Salt – 1 tsp.

- Stevia – 1 tsp.

- Black pepper – 1/8 tsp.

- Egg yolks – 2

- Olive oil – 1 ¾ cups, divided

- Vinegar – 2 tbsp.

Method

1. Fill a large bowl with ice. Nestle a medium bowl into the ice.

2. To the bowl, add the mustard powder, 1 tbsp. lemon juice, salt, stevia, and pepper. Beat well with a hand mixer.

3. Add the egg yolks, mix well on medium-high speed.

4. Very slowly, while continuing to mix, add ¼ cup olive oil, tsp. by tsp. Slowly continue to add the remaining 1 ½ cups of oil while mixing steadily.

5. When the mixture begins to thicken, continue mixing and add the vinegar and the remaining tbsp. of lemon juice intermittently with the oil.

6. Continue until all the oil has been used.

Nutritional Facts Per Serving (1 tbsp.)

- Calories: 110

- Fat: 12.3g

- Carb: 0.1g

- Protein: 0.2g

Hollandaise Sauce

Prep Time: 10 minutes

Cook Time: 0 minutes

Serving: 8

Ingredients

- Egg yolks – 2

- Salt – ¼ tsp.

- Butter – ½ cup, melted

- Lemon juice – 1 tbsp.

Method

1. To a bowl, add the egg yolks and beat with a hand mixer until they are thick and lemon-colored. Add the salt.

2. While continuing to beat, slowly add the butter, 1 tsp. at a time, alternating with the lemon juice, ½ tsp. at a time. Beat until sauce is smooth.

Nutritional Facts Per Serving (1 tbsp.)

- Calories: 116

- Fat: 12.7g

- Carb: 0.2g

- Protein: 0.8g

Mustard Shallot Vinaigrette

Prep Time: 5 minutes

Cook Time: 0 minutes

Serving: 8

Ingredients

- Olive oil – ½ cup

- Apple cider vinegar – ½ cup

- Dijon mustard – 3 tbsp.

- Shallot – 1, minced

- Salt – ½ tsp.

- Ground black pepper – ¼ tsp.

Method

1. Combine everything in a blender and blend until combined.

Nutritional Facts Per Serving (1 tbsp.)

- Calories: 117

- Fat: 12.8g

- Carb: 0.9g

- Protein: 0.3g

Pasta Sauce

Prep Time: 5 minutes

Cook Time: 10 minutes

Serving: 8

Ingredients

- Diced tomatoes – 3 cups

- Olive oil – ¼ cup

- Minced garlic – 2 tbsp.

- Chopped fresh basil – 1 tbsp.

- Onion powder – 1 tsp.

- Crushed red pepper flakes -1 tsp.

- Salt – ½ tsp.

- Ground black pepper to taste – ¼ tsp.

Method

1. In a food processor, add the tomatoes and pulse once or twice so the tomatoes still have texture.

2. In a saucepan over medium heat, heat the olive oil for 1 minute. Add the garlic and cook for 1 minute.

3. Add the basil, tomatoes, onion powder, red pepper flakes, salt, and pepper to the saucepan. Whisk to combine.

4. Bring the mixture to a simmer and cook for 10 minutes.

5. Cool and store in the refrigerator.

Nutritional Facts Per Serving (1 tbsp.)

• Calories: 69

• Fat: 6.5g

• Carb: 2.5g

• Protein: 0.7g

Pizza Sauce

Prep Time: 5 minutes

Cook Time: 12 minutes

Serving: 16

Ingredients

- Diced tomatoes – 2 cups

- Olive oil – ¼ cup

- Chopped onion – ¼ cup

- Minced garlic – 2 tbsp.

- Tomato paste – 1 cup, no sugar added

- Onion powder – 2 tsp.

- Crushed red pepper flakes – 1 tsp.

- Salt – ½ tsp.

- Ground black pepper – ¼ tsp.

- Chopped fresh basil – 3 tbsp.

Method

1. Add the tomatoes in a food processor and pulse twice so the tomatoes still have texture.

2. In a saucepan, heat the olive oil for 1 minute.

3. Add the garlic and onion and cook for 2 minutes.

4. Add the tomato paste, tomatoes, onion powder, red pepper flakes, salt, and pepper to the saucepan. Stir to combine.

5. Bring to a simmer and cook for 10 minutes.

6. Remove from the heat and cool.

7. Add the basil and stir to mix.

Nutritional Facts Per Serving (1 tbsp.)

• Calories: 46

• Fat: 3.3g

• Carb: 3.4g

• Protein: 0.9g

Pesto Sauce

Prep Time: 5 minutes

Cook Time: 0 minutes

Serving: 14

Ingredients

- Fresh basil – 4 cups, chopped

- Olive oil – ½ cup

- Pine nuts – 1/3 cups

- Garlic – 2 cloves, minced

- Grated Parmesan cheese – ¼ cup

- Grated pecorino cheese – ¼ cup

- Salt – 1 tsp.

Method

1. In a food processor, add the olive oil, basil, pine nuts, and garlic.

2. Pulse in short bursts while slowly adding the Parmesan and pecorino cheeses.

3. Add the salt, and blend until smooth.

4. Store.

Nutritional Facts Per Serving (1 tbsp.)

- Calories: 106

- Fat: 10.9g

- Carb: 0.9g

- Protein: 2.6g

Taco Seasoning

Prep Time: 4 minutes

Cook Time: 0 minutes

Makes: 2/3 cup

Ingredients

- Chili powder – ¼ cup

- Ground cumin – 1 ½ tbsp.

- Fine sea salt – 1 tbsp.

- Fresh ground black pepper – 1 tbsp.

- Swerve confectioners' or monk fruit – 1 tbsp.

- Paprika – 2 tsp. (optional)

- Red pepper flakes – 1 tsp.

- Garlic powder – 1 tsp.

- Onion powder – 1 tsp.

- Dried ground oregano – 1 tsp.

- Ground coriander – 1 tsp.

Method

1. Place all ingredients in a jar and shake until well combined.

2. Store.

Nutritional Facts Per Serving (1 ¼ tsp.)

- Calories: 8

- Fat: 0.3g

- Carb: 1.3g

- Protein: 0.3g

Pizza Spice Mix

Prep Time: 3 minutes

Cook Time: 0 minutes

Makes: ½ cup

Ingredients

- Grated Parmesan cheese – ¼ cup

- Garlic powder – 3 tbsp.

- Onion powder – 1 tbsp.

- Dried oregano leaves – 1 tbsp.

Method

1. Place all ingredients in a jar and shake well to combine.

2. Store.

Nutritional Facts Per Serving (2 tbsp.)

- Calories: 60

- Fat: 2.4g

- Carb: 6.7g

- Protein: 4.4g

Mayonnaise II

Prep Time: 5 minutes

Cook Time: 0 minutes

Makes: 1 ½ cup

Ingredients

- Egg yolks – 2 large

- Lemon juice – 2 tsp.

- MCT oil or avocado oil – 1 cup

- Dijon mustard – 1 tbsp.

- Fine sea salt – ½ tsp.

Method

1. Place the ingredients in the order listed in a jar.

2. Place the immersion blender at the bottom of the jar.

3. Blend very slowly and move the blender to the top.

4. Store.

Nutritional Facts Per Serving

- Calories: 92

- Fat: 10g

- Carb: 0.1g

- Protein: 0.3g

Almond Milk

Prep Time: 10 minutes

Cook Time: 0 minutes

Servings: 6 (1 cup serving)

Ingredients

• Skinless raw almonds – ½ cup

• Filtered water – 6 cups, plus 1 cup more if soaking nuts

• Vanilla extract – ½ tsp. optional

• Liquid stevia – 2 drops

• Pinch of sea salt

Method

1. Soak the nuts in 1 cup water. Refrigerate overnight.

2. Drain and place the nuts in a blender. Add 6 cups of water, stevia, vanilla, and salt and puree until smooth.

3. Strain and store the milk.

4. You can use the strained nuts to blend again and make more milk.

Nutritional Facts Per Serving

- Calories: 69

- Fat: 6g

- Carb: 2.6g

- Protein: 2.5g

Holiday Gravy

Prep Time: 5 minutes

Cook Time: 10 to 25 minutes

Servings: 6

Ingredients

- Dried porcini mushrooms – ½ cup

- Filtered water – 1 cup

- Unsalted butter – ½ cup

- Garlic - clove, minced

- Pan drippings from turkey or beef roast

- Turkey or chicken bone broth – 2 cups

- Coconut flour – 1 tbsp.

- Heavy whipping cream or coconut milk – ¼ cup

- Dijon mustard – 1 tsp.

- Fine sea salt – 1 tsp.

- Pinch of black or white peppercorns

- Fresh thyme – 2 sprigs

Method

1. In a small bowl, combine the mushrooms and water. Let sit for 10 to 15 minutes. Drain and chop the mushrooms.

2. In a medium saucepan over low heat, melt the butter. Simmer until lightly browned.

3. Add the garlic and cook for 1 to 2 minutes. Add the pan drippings. Add mushrooms and stir well to combine.

4. Whisk in the broth, then add the coconut flour. Whisk until well blended.

5. Simmer over low heat for 5 to 20 minutes.

6. Remove from the heat and add the mustard, cream, salt, peppercorns, and thyme sprigs.

7. Blend with a hand mixer until smooth.

8. Strain and serve.

Nutritional Facts Per Serving

• Calories: 263

• Fat: 27.5g

• Carb: 1g

• Protein: 2.8g

Conclusion

Insulin resistance is one of the most widespread health problems affecting western culture. If you have developed insulin resistance and struggling with weight loss, then you are not alone. According to recent data, as many as 1 in 3 Americans could develop insulin resistance if they don't stop unhealthy eating habits and lifestyles. This insulin resistance guidebook is not a simple diet book – it is an eating guide and shows you that you can reverse insulin resistance without expensive drugs or surgery. A little knowledge, education, following the right diet, and a few lifestyle changes can help you reverse insulin resistance.

Recipes Index

Chapter 5: Breakfast Recipes _____ 38

Breakfast Muffins _____ 38

Vegetable Breakfast Bread _____ 40

Avocado Muffins _____ 42

Cheese and Oregano Muffins _____ 44

Turkey Breakfast _____ 46

Breakfast Hash _____ 48

Brussels Sprout Delight _____ 50

Chia Pudding _____ 52

Hemp Porridge _____ 54

Simple Breakfast Cereal _____ 56

Egg Porridge _____ 58

Pancakes _____ 60

Almond Pancakes _____ 62

French Toast _____ 64

Waffles _____ 67

Chapter 6: Lunch Recipes _____ 69

Zucchini Boats _____ 69

Chicken Sandwich _____ 71

Tuna Bites with Avocado _____ 74

Sausage and Pepper Soup _____ 76

Chicken Nuggets_____ 78

Cauliflower Rice with Chicken _____ 80

Chicken and Bacon Casserole _____ 82

Mexican Casserole _____ 84

Almond Pizza_____ 86

Chicken Thighs _____ 88

Grilled Cheese Sandwich _____ 90

Crisp Pizza _____ 92

Meatballs with Bacon and Cheese _____ 94

Sausage & Cabbage Skillet Melt _____ 96

Kung Pao Chicken _____ 98

Chapter 7: Side Dish Recipes _____ **101**

Simple Kimchi _____ 101

Oven-fried Green Beans _____ 103

Cauliflower Mash _____ 105

Portobello Mushrooms _____ 107

Pesto_____ 109

Brussels Sprouts and Bacon _____ 111

Avocado Fries _____ 113

Mushroom and Spinach _____115

Okra and Tomatoes _____117

Collard Greens with Turkey _____119

Eggplant and Tomatoes_____121

Broccoli with Lemon Almond Butter _____123

Sautéed Broccoli _____125

Greek Side Salad _____127

Summer Side Salad _____129

Chapter 8: Snack and Appetizer Recipes_____**131**

Marinated Eggs _____131

Onion and Cauliflower Dip _____133

Pesto Crackers _____135

Pumpkin Muffins_____137

Tortilla Chips _____139

Jalapeno Balls_____141

Pepperoni Bombs_____143

Cheeseburger Muffins _____145

Pizza Dip_____148

Flaxseed and Almond Muffins _____150

Fried Queso _____152

Maple and Pecan Bars_____154

Baked Chia Seeds _____157

Avocado Dip _____159

Prosciutto Wrapped Shrimp _____161

Chapter 9: Fish and Seafood Recipes_____**163**

Shrimp and Cucumber Noodle Salad _____163

Roasted Mahi Mahi and Tomato _____165

Spicy Shrimp _____168

Shrimp Stew _____170

Garlicky Mussels_____172

Fried Calamari with Spicy Sauce _____174

Octopus Salad_____176

Clam Chowder _____178

Salmon Rolls _____180

Salmon Skewers _____182

Cod Salad _____184

Sardine Salad _____186

Italian Clam Delight _____188

Lemon-Glazed Salmon _____190

Tuna and Chimichurri Sauce_____192

Chapter 10: Poultry Recipes _____**195**

Creamy Chicken _____195

Chicken and Broccoli Casserole _____197

Creamy Chicken Soup _____199

Four-Cheese Chicken _____201

Crusted Chicken _____203

Orange Chicken _____205

Bacon-Wrapped Chicken _____208

Turkey Sushi _____210

Bacon Wrapped Turkey Meatballs _____212

Turkey, Avocado, and Umami Wraps _____215

Crispy Duck Legs with Braised Vegetables _____217

Roasted Duck in Wine Sauce _____219

Chinese Duck with Orange Sauce _____221

Chicken with Olive Tapenade _____224

Baked Turkey Delight _____226

Chapter 11: Meat Recipes _____228

Roasted Pork Belly _____228

Stuffed Pork_____230

Lemon and Garlic Pork _____233

Jamaican Pork_____235

Juicy Pork Chops _____237

Beef Patties _____239

Beef Meatballs Casserole _____ 241

Beef and Tomato-Stuffed Squash _____ 244

Beef Goulash _____ 246

Braised Lamb Chops _____ 248

Lamb Salad _____ 251

Moroccan Lamb _____ 254

Lamb Curry _____ 257

Lamb Stew_____ 259

Sausage Stew _____ 261

Chapter 12: Vegetable Recipes _____ **263**

Arugula and Broccoli Soup _____ 263

Zucchini Cream_____ 265

Zucchini and Avocado Soup_____ 267

Swiss Chard Salad _____ 269

Catalan-Style Greens _____ 271

Fried Parmesan Tomatoes _____ 273

Creamy "mac"-n-Cheese _____ 275

Brown Butter Mushrooms _____ 278

Creamy coleslaw_____ 280

Onion Rings _____ 282

Avocado Fries II _____ 284

Chapter 13: Dessert Recipes _____ **286**

Peanut Butter and Chocolate Brownies _____ 286

Blueberry Scones _____ 288

Chocolate Cookies _____ 290

Peach Cake _____ 292

Lemon Custard _____ 294

Caramel Custard _____ 296

Coconut Granola _____ 298

Peanut Butter and Chia Pudding _____ 300

No-Bake Cookies _____ 302

Tiramisu Pudding _____ 304

Cherry and Chia Jam _____ 306

Almond Truffles _____ 308

Raspberry and Coconut Dessert _____ 310

Vanilla Parfaits _____ 312

Creamy Coconut Pudding _____ 314

Chapter 14: Condiments, Sauces, Dressings ____ **316**

Barbecue Sauce _____ 316

Teriyaki Sauce _____ 319

Sugar-Free Ketchup _____ 321

Blue Cheese Sauce _____ 323

Ranch Dressing _____ 325

Mustard Cream Sauce _____ 327

Homemade Mayonnaise _____ 329

Hollandaise Sauce _____ 331

Mustard Shallot Vinaigrette _____ 333

Pasta Sauce _____ 335

Pizza Sauce _____ 337

Pesto Sauce _____ 339

Taco Seasoning _____ 341

Pizza Spice Mix _____ 343

Mayonnaise II _____ 344

Almond Milk _____ 346

Holiday Gravy _____ 348

www.ingramcontent.com/pod-product-compliance
Lightning Source LLC
LaVergne TN
LVHW022145020125
800342LV00006B/98